PRAISE FOR *PEDAGOGY AS ENCOUNTER*

"How do we teach and learn? Is teaching an instruction, an activism, or is it an encounter in which both 'teacher' and 'student' learn? In this wonderful book of 120 stories of encounters Naeem Inayatullah restores 'teaching' to a human plane of interaction and discovery." — **Stephen Chan**, OBE, SOAS University of London

"I think of Inayatullah in this book as our modern day gadfly of pedagogy. Or he's Diogenes of Sinope relaxing at the feet of Alexander the Great, who has asked him what he might desire above all else, to which he replies, for you to step away you're blocking the sun. What's blocking the sun in this inquiry are pat, self-congratulatory paeans to the joys of teaching. Maybe not with Diogenes's derision, but the same fearlessness is here, the same subversive spirit, ever-searching for authentic answers to what we are to our students. What do they really learn? And whatever that is, how much, really, is it from anything we do or say? This is a loving, brilliant, and brave exploration." —**Cory Brown**, Writing Professor and author of five books of poems, the latest *A Long Slow Climb*

"An extraordinary book that refuses to tell us how to teach but instead takes us by the hand through an encounter with the author, his students, and his remarkable method, honed across decades in the classroom. The book's challenge extends far beyond pedagogy to our very grasp of being and shows what a life that accepts the gift of impossibility might be. If, as mine does, your heart rebels against much it contains, the book will not let you escape the question of why. Read it if you dare." —**Jenny Edkins**, The University of Manchester and author of *Change and the Politics of Certainty*

"Few scholars of International Relations have considered teaching as a practice of international politics rather than as a conveyor of disciplinary wisdom. For Naeem Inayatullah, the impulse to teach is a puzzle, an imperial gesture at that, and not a vocation or a mission. Through beautiful autobiographical vignettes—odes to his students, teachers, and colleagues—Inayatullah demonstrates in this book what openings can be created if teaching were treated as an encounter and not a mere pedagogical tool." —**Aida Hozic**, University of Florida

"All of us who wear the label 'teacher' should strive to be as thoughtful about its meaning as Naeem is. These deeply evocative personal narratives challenge us to disassemble the professor/student antinomy, to ground the agency of learning where it belongs, and to live out our pedagogical convictions in the classroom environments for which we are responsible." —**Jamie Freuh**, Bridgewater University

"Inayatullah's book is a demonstration of immanence, the bringing together of everyone and everything into the experience of learning. In this series of vignettes, like a great piece of music, all the pieces fit together and support each other. Take one away or break the parts up, and the whole no longer exists. Try to put your finger on, or pin down, or name it, and you've immediately lost it. It's the circling around the subject that reveals its shape. As Inayatullah shows, this is also what happens in the classroom when teachers let go of the desire to teach, and instead create a more hopeful space for encounter and healing." —**Andrea Paras**, University of Guelph

"Naeem Inayatullah takes us on his journey of pedagogical risks, frustrations and all, undoing goals like teaching and learning to make space for encounter. He takes encounter seriously, not as serendipity but as method, recognizing how everyone's insatiable curiosity is entangled in resistance to learn from teachers, who are imperialists. Naeem Inayatullah turns teaching into listening . . . and pedagogy on its head. 'Anything might happen if we treat pedagogy as encounter.' Worth the adventure." —**Manuela L. Picq**, Amherst College

"You may not be ready for the central premise in *Pedagogy as Encounter*—teaching is impossible, learning is unlikely—but read it anyway. Naeem Inayatullah's stories stay with you. They speak to you and say something different every time. And it is not because they are beautifully written, although they are. It is because he is willing to share something of himself, thereby inviting us to seek something of ourselves that we might be willing to share." —**Harmonie Toros**, University of Kent

"This book is both a moving teaching memoir and a thoughtful and original reflection on meta-pedagogical issues by a great International

Relations scholar who has more than 30 years of teaching experience and has produced pioneering work on pedagogy, narrative forms of writing, and autobiography in IR. While most of the works about teaching IR are interested in how teaching and learning can be made more effective (according to different objectives), this book engages with the question of whether teaching and learning are possible at all. Dr. Inayatullah's rigorous and generous reflections on the purpose of teaching will be of interest to International Relations scholars and students and to anyone who teaches and learns (which is all of us, as the author says)." —**Paula Sandrin**, Pontifical Catholic University of Rio

"This is a courageous confrontation of colonial counter-insurgency in the classroom. Naeem Inayatullah's refusal to pacify either himself or his students unearths vital resources not only for enlivening our learning spaces, but also for living well with otherness, both of ourselves and of others." —**Narendran Kumarakulasingam**, Conrad Grebel University College, Canada

"If we accept the premise that teaching and learning are impossible, then what happens in the classroom? *Pedagogy as Encounter: Beyond the Teaching Imperative* is a book about one educator's high-stakes experiments in how to be in relation to his students without domination, imposition, or expectation. The book is a series of stories and vignettes of radical openness to encounter, grounded in political philosophy, that are brimming with doubt, risk, tension, humor, and love. This is not just a book about teaching. It is, thinking analogically, a book about how to be in the world." —**Lori Leonard**, Cornell University

"The terms curiosity and meaning acquire a special tonality and richness in the 'pedagogical encounters' that Naeem Inayatullah so deftly scrutinizes in this account. Premised on over four decades of teaching and learning, there is a palpable self-reflexivity and welcome candour in ample evidence on every page here when Inayatuallah probes the depths of the possible and the impossible in these interconnected realms. Anyone who cares about teaching must take a dip into this pond and not hesitate to get drenched intellectually and affectively in the best sense of the term." —**Siddharth Mallavarapu**, Shiv Nadar University

"Teaching's claim to innocent education is only outmatched by its emancipatory heroics. In this book, Naeem challenges both self-images by boldly proposing that 'teaching is impossible and learning is unlikely.' At once a theoretical work on pedagogy and imperialism, and the narrative of a path of abandoning hopes of both conventional and liberation pedagogies, this book is an implicating confession that can neither be dismissed nor accepted without grave implications to our work as educators. In exchange, it offers a bottomless source of inspiration and energy for those trailing the teaching journey." —**Paulo Chamon**, Pontifical Catholic University of Rio

"These evocative confessions trace a life in the classroom via richly woven tapestries of encounter. Insisting on the impossibility of learning and teaching, these meditations upend easy narratives of knowledge transfer or liberatory education and embrace instead the difficult pedagogical work of co-presence. Important, provocative, and moving, this book's strength lies in its vulnerability: readers bear witness to the frustration, anger, shame, joy, laughter, and love that accompany a pedagogy of encounter and emergence." —**Kate Schick**, Victoria University of Wellington

"I love this book. Rich with personal vignettes and deep theoretical insight, this book offers an honest account of teaching that serves to inspire. Professor Inayatullah calls on us to critically think about our vocation as teachers. By placing his encounters with his students as inspirational moments for self-reflection, Inayatullah demonstrates the ups and downs, the challenges, and the wonderous moments of teaching. *Pedagogy as Encounter* is a must read for anybody teaching in a university environment." —**Ilan Zvi Baron**, Durham University

"*Pedagogy as Encounter* offers us the rarest of gifts: a method for inhabiting a profession whose purpose is to support and excuse Empire. By exposing teaching's complicity in the imperial project, Inayatullah guides us through critique as a process of our own un-doing. His courage in exposing himself returns to us the negative as a resource, as a gift for us to open. This is a work of fierce compassion, built on the rift of our crushed hope and sustained with the critical love that both ruptures and liberates us." —**Lori Amy**, Georgia Southern University

Pedagogy as Encounter

CREATIVE INTERVENTIONS IN GLOBAL POLITICS
Series Editors:
Shine Choi, Cristina Masters, Swati Parashar, and Marysia Zalewski

The landscape of contemporary global politics is complex and often-times violent. Yet the urgency to provide solutions or immediate practical actions to this violence oftentimes leads to inadequate knowledge. This is despite the abundance of theoretical, conceptual, and methodological tools available—much of this produced through conventional academic disciplines, notably International Relations, Political Theory, and Philosophy. But the constraints imposed on these traditional disciplines profoundly limit their ability to incorporate and make effective use of more creative and innovative methodologies found in other disciplines and genres.

This series provides a unique opportunity to offer creative intellectual space to work with an eclectic and rich range of disciplines and approaches, including performative methodologies, storytelling, narrative and auto-ethnography, embodied research methodologies, participant research, visual and film methodologies, and arts-based methodologies.

Titles in the Series

Pedagogy as Encounter

Beyond the Teaching Imperative

Naeem Inayatullah

ROWMAN & LITTLEFIELD
Lanham • Boulder • New York • London

Published by Rowman & Littlefield
An imprint of The Rowman & Littlefield Publishing Group, Inc.
4501 Forbes Boulevard, Suite 200, Lanham, Maryland 20706
www.rowman.com

86-90 Paul Street, London EC2A 4NE

British Library Cataloguing in Publication Information Available

Library of Congress Cataloging-in-Publication Data

Names: Inayatullah, Naeem, author.
Title: Pedagogy as encounter : beyond the teaching imperative / Naeem
   Inayatullah.
Description: First edition. | Lanham, Maryland : Rowman & Littlefield,
   2022. | Series: Creative interventions in global politics | Includes
   bibliographical references and index.
Identifiers: LCCN 2021061836 (print) | LCCN 2021061837 (ebook) | ISBN
   9781538165119 (cloth) | ISBN 9781538165133 (paperback) | ISBN
   9781538165126 (ebook)
Subjects: LCSH: Reflective teaching. | Teacher-student relationships. |
   Teachers—Professional relationships. | Classroom management.
Classification: LCC LB1025.3 .I455 2022 (print) | LCC LB1025.3 (ebook) |
   DDC 371.14/4—dc23/eng/20220124
LC record available at https://lccn.loc.gov/2021061836
LC ebook record available at https://lccn.loc.gov/2021061837

Contents

CHAPTER 1

Prologue

The Encounter

I believed that teaching and learning were possible when I began my career. Nothing in my socialization or education suggested otherwise. I may have had doubts, but if I did, I ignored them to fend off confusion, paralysis, and joblessness. And even if some part of me sensed the impossibility of my venture, why did I treat doubt as a threat and not also as a resource, as a gift to open?

Sven Lindqvist hints at the answer in his exquisite *Exterminate the Brutes*, in which he claims progress comes at the cost of genocide. He ends with the mesmerizing lines, "You already know this. So do I. It is not knowledge we lack. What is missing is the courage to understand what we know and draw conclusions." Lindqvist claims knowing requires courage of the kind that most of us cannot usually muster. How then did *he* face down his fear of knowing? How might we do the same? In suggesting that all we need is courage, Lindqvist sidesteps a question: Why don't we have the courage that knowing and acting require?

My subject is not progress and genocide but teaching and learning.[1] In homage to Lindqvist, I could offer corresponding lines: "Teaching is impossible. Learning is unlikely. Encounter is the remainder. You already know this, as do I. It is not knowledge we lack. What is missing is the courage to understand and draw conclusions." But homage

---

1. My purview is limited to teaching and learning as they occur in Western formal educational institutions. I suspect that my claims are generalizable to other cultures, alternative institutions, informal spaces, and everyday life processes. Nevertheless, developing that wider scope is a challenge for a different book.

derives from respect, and respect demands critique: I want to turn his lines as one does a crystal, to see what else we might see.

Why don't we have the courage that knowing and acting require? In response, I offer a largely confessional narrative that turns the issue of courage into a question of the gains and losses that accrue when we give up on trying to teach and, instead, follow a pedagogy of encounter and emergence. I ask, *If we treat teaching as if it were impossible and learning as unlikely, what can we find in the classroom?* I do not suggest that we surrender to teaching's difficulty by abdicating our responsibility. Rather, I wonder, *What emerges if we vacate teaching and learning as explicit goals?*

The answer, it turns out, is *plenty*. This book describes that *plenty* and how to discover it.

* * *

Later in my life, I discovered the *tragic sensibility*—the stance that one finds creativity and a kind of freedom, by first accepting the impossibility of any given situation.

As a graduate student, I struggled with Marx and Hegel and discovered that reading the British philosopher R. G. Collingwood's interpretations of Hegel served me well. I read everything I could find by Collingwood. In his *The Idea of History*, Collingwood discusses this phrase: "The present is perfect."[2]

Collingwood points out that this does not mean we live in the best of worlds, it does not mean that things cannot be better, and it does not mean that we have no option but to celebrate or support the status quo. It means only that, given past problems, the present condition of the world is already the best solution humans have derived. This reasoning grounds me.

"The present is perfect" proposition moves me to appreciate the intricacy of past troubles. It humbles me into accepting the sincerity and determination of those whose attempts to solve past problems have led to our current predicaments. It shifts my attention from our failure in finding solutions to grasping the deeper intractability of our difficulties.

---

2. Collingwood, R. G. (1962). *The Idea of History* (Oxford: Clarendon Press), Part III, Sec. 5.

It is but a short step from an appreciation of the intractability of problems to consider their impossibility.

Consider, then, what I call the "impossibility theorem." Problems are so complex and so overwritten with multiple values, it is best to consider them impossible. Of course, it follows that if the problem is impossible, then the solution is unlikely.

When confronted with the impossibility theorem, some react with despondency, depression, or denial. I find this fully understandable, but it is also a method of denying our resources. If our actions are to be meaningful in the long run, then better to comprehend the impossibility of a problem than to minimize it, or to wish away its difficulty. Facing the impossible can give us a lifetime of energy, courage, and stamina. Moreover, it can give us the daring to search for alternatives. How? Let me answer with a quote from Henry Kariel, who writes, "When exits close and options are cancelled our vision is suddenly sharpened and we can catch ourselves in the act of seeing. An auspicious moment for educators."[3]

Thus, for our purposes, the idea of impossibility would be accepting that such goals as the widespread implementation of civic education, a material commitment to diversity, and engagement with democratic processes are not realistic. Paradoxically, we may understand that *this* is a better starting point than our usual complicity in the imperialism of teaching projects.

It follows, then, that the fundamental assumption of teaching, whether in a classroom or in a national or global political arena, must be that no one wants to learn. From this premise, we arrive at an infinitely fertile question: How do you teach when you accept that no one wants to learn? What strategies do you bring to the classroom? Conversation? Demonstration? Presentation?

I confess that everything changed for me once I internalized the proposition that my students don't want to learn.

We can ask, why does no one want to learn? Once we force ourselves to ask this question, the answers come at us from every direction. Learning, as a student in a class or as a citizen within a society, has consequences. It ruptures the self, alienates us from our families

---

3. Kariel, Henry. (1977). "Becoming Political," in *Teaching Political Science*, ed. Vernon van Dyke (London: Humanities Press), p. 129.

and communities, and threatens the national identity. Often, it's simply not worth the risk.

However, if the principle *no one wants to learn* stands on its own, without a counterweight or opposite, we do *not yet* have an impossible situation. Thus, its opposite must be present.

The counter principle, the assumption that informs our educational system and notions of a participatory democracy and a civil society, is that we are driven by a desire to satiate our curiosity, to make our life meaningful, to come to an accurate understanding of the actual world, and to connect with each other at some deeper level. And this hidden and subordinate but nevertheless powerful desire presents possibilities—possibilities that I explore in this book.

In sum, *No one wants to learn, but everyone has an insatiable curiosity*. This paradox has greater explanatory power, and one of them without the other avoids the fertility of impossibility.

* * *

My research portrays European colonial imperialism as encounters dominated by pedagogical projects. For Europeans, Third World others are part of the human family who have lost their way, fallen behind, and need Western tutelage. Early in my career, I began to draw parallels between my theoretical and pedagogical work. As I examined sixteenth-century encounters between Spanish conquistadors and the Amerindians, nineteenth-century British colonialism in India, and contemporary US foreign policy in Iraq, I began to think of these colonialisms as teaching projects.

Teachers are imperialists. They think they know what is best for others because they have knowledge that others are denied and from which others can benefit. This "exclusive knowledge,"[4] together with less disinterested motives, drives the wish to teach. The extraction of gold, oil, and resources fuels colonial engagement, but imperialists also need to believe in their own goodness. The Spanish understood the conversion of Amerindians to Christianity as their responsibility to Indians, the British believed themselves to be enlightening the subcontinent

---

4. Inayatullah, Naeem. (2019). "Why Do Some People Think They Know What is Best for Others?" in *Global Politics: A New Introduction, 3rd Edition*, eds. Jenny Edkins and Maja Zehfuss (London: Routledge), pp. 430–53.

with Western rationality, and the United States considers itself to be the creator of liberal democracies for the good of the world.

Exclusive knowledge has a positive side because all of us have some kind of special insight that we feel obliged to share. Yet, it is almost always the case that exclusive knowledge leads us not into encounters among equals but instead into the pedagogical imposition, the impulse to teach. Imperialism, especially modern imperialism, is not just born from the profit motive. It emerges as well from the need to feel as if one's exclusive knowledge is, in fact, exclusive. You prove exceptionality by finding a lack in the other, which you fill with your special knowledge. When others become your replicas, you are satisfied that, in fact, you were right all along and that you are a particular and singular being.

The impulse for encounter is the opposite. It derives from a loneliness, which, paradoxically, comes from the same place as the teaching drive. The lack that the imperialist fills by making replicas of himself, simultaneously projects an emptiness and vulnerability that others can see and feel. This contradictory project simmers in the teacher and in the imperialist. On the one hand is the projection of exclusivity (and superiority), but on the other hand is a simultaneous projection of lack—an absence of love, of being in the world with others. Imperialist cultures, as in the United States, can be perceived in this twofold way, but so can my own role in the classroom.

Even if we take imperialists on their own terms as misunderstood providers of public goods, their pedagogical projects largely produce resentment and rejection in their target populations. Imposition is the problem. For me, the question became, "Can we imagine mutually beneficial encounters without imposition?"

In the classroom, the teacher occupies the position of the imperialist. Students play the role of Third World others. The teacher determines the grades and controls the interactions with students. We impose, for their own good, of course. The parallel is not exact, but there is enough of an overlap to ask: Can we create "authority without domination"[5] in the classroom? If we can, would it be scalable to the larger world? Just

5. A phrase provided by my former student, Sue Lambe, after reading early drafts of this manuscript.

how far away can pedagogy move from imposition? Far, as it turns out, but not without significant risk.

* * *

Allow me to zoom out and expose the frame.

Thucydides, like the rest of the ancient Greeks, believed in a cyclic theory of history. I read his famous Melian Dialogue as a confession about the impossibility of history, that while we can uncover the patterns of history, we cannot change them.

And yet, Thucydides is compelled to share this confession with us.

Adam Smith believes that the public good appears when individuals pursue their self-interest. There is little need then for citizens to learn or for the state to teach. The gap between the interests of citizens and the public good is filled by the providential workings of the invisible hand.

Hegel, who is a student of Smith and the Scottish Enlightenment, believes in human learning, not the invisible hand. The purpose of markets, he says, is to teach citizens of a commercial society that they need the state. Self-interest begets public ethics, not automatically but through a process of struggle and social strife. And always, too late.

I mention these titans of Western political theory because their work can be read as a commentary on the possibilities of learning and teaching or, more accurately, on the process through which knowing and learning come into being, if they come into being at all.

So, when we discuss classroom problems and classroom processes, such as civic education and democracy, we are right in the middle of central questions of political philosophy. Further, as we examine the impossibilities of teaching and learning, we are never far from the impossibilities of life itself.

I don't need to be correct about these claims. I wish only to highlight our usual prohibition on the theorizing of teaching.

* * *

Which still leaves one important question: What is in this for me? What is in this for the teacher?

Students don't learn what we teach them. If they learn, it is not content but form. How does the teacher relate to learning materials? How does the teacher approach text, theory, current events? How do teachers express their own curiosity? How do teachers convey their own desire? How do teachers externalize the questions that fuel their own bodies?

What is in it for the teachers is the potential overlap between their own desire and the desire of the students.

In this way, we are already intrinsic collaborators, even as one is an apprentice and the other the master. Teachers are not meant to be masters of content. Rather, we convey how one might align oneself to desire, to curiosity, to a search for knowledge and healing.

CHAPTER 2

Motivations

Origins, Memory, Family, and Political Economy

I am the first-born son of parents whose own parents toiled in the fields of the Punjab. My family genealogy is tied to small-scale rice farming. My parents' journey from these origins to the larger world is nothing short of miraculous, and my work tries to grasp this miracle.

As an undergraduate, I studied international development. After completing my master's in agricultural economics, I applied for jobs at various international institutions, such as the International Monetary Fund and the Asian Development Bank. The World Bank encouraged me to pursue a PhD and then re-apply. I set out to do just that at the Graduate School of International Studies at the University of Denver, but my plans changed as I went through my doctoral program.

* * *

In 1960, I was a four-year-old living in Peshawar, Pakistan, where my father was a village researcher at the Academy for Rural Development. The Academy was a Ford Foundation-funded project whose upper management was comprised of professors from Michigan State University. It was one of the scores of development missions spread through Latin America, Africa, and Asia as a hedge against communist influence and a beacon to a future foretold by Western social science. A few miles west of the Academy is the Khyber Pass, and nearby is Bareder Air Base from which Gary Powers flew his U-2 spy flights over the Soviet Union. That same year, I listened to the older boys argue about cars while leaning on the red brick wall that enclosed the small yards of the tidy bungalows rented to the local professional staff.

A few boys claimed that Lincoln Continentals were the best, and others touted Cadillacs. Turning away, I looked up to see a plane slowly drift away, perhaps on the same path as Powers' U-2, just months before.

Today, the Academy still functions, and Bareder Air Base is no mere remnant of the past. From 1922 to 1940, Royal Air Force Station Peshawar provided support to British army units that included field regiments near the Afghanistan border. The United States utilized this base in the early years of the Cold War after the British passed the torch of Empire to their Anglo brothers. More recently, following the attack of September 11, 2001, in New York City, the base was one of five airfields considered by US and Pakistani military representatives as suitable for staging US vengeance against Al-Qaeda and Afghanistan. As far as I know, it went unused. Still, in the dark of night, my five-year-old nephew in Karachi would pull his pillow over his ears in a futile attempt to muffle the city-shaking rumble caused by the rows of US planes on their way from the Indian Ocean island of Diego Garcia to Mazār-i-Sharīf, Kandahar, and countless other targets. When I think of him there, the past erupts.

My father owned a black Volkswagen Bug. It was his proudest possession and a rare sight on the roads of Peshawar, which contained all wonder of human and animal traffic but few cars. The singularity of my father's VW was such that I could not imagine how a Lincoln Continental might be better. I supposed this memory of cars has something to do with the first films I ever saw—films of fire engines on the outdoor screens within the Academy compound, screens depicting courageous firefighters skillfully deploying ladders, hoses, and pressured columns of seemingly solid water. I had never imagined such wonders. Where was this place with these amazing figures? It had to be somewhere far. The nearest portal to this other world was the Academy, with its clean-edged, cooled, cemented architecture and ice-cold water fountains every few hundred feet.

Sometimes I long for that life to have been as perfect as it seemed at the time. I want to keep my faith in a steady climb towards the tangible summit of developmental progress, if for no other reason than to explain my apparently random trajectory from Peshawar to Bloomington, Indiana, where my father studied; to New York City, Geneva, and Kuala Lumpur, where he worked for the United Nations; to East

Lansing, Michigan, and Denver, Colorado, where I studied; to Boulder, Colorado, and Syracuse, New York, where I taught; and to Ithaca, New York, where I have been teaching for the last twenty-four years.

In my thirty-four-year career, I have taught courses in four areas: global political economy;[1] international relations;[2] political theory;[3] and culture.[4] All these courses are designed to provide a global and historical context in which students can locate themselves. And they are designed to demonstrate how Third World states exist in a paradoxical condition that combines material paucity and cultural abundance.

* * *

Judith Turner was the assistant principal at the Lycée des Nations when I was in eighth grade in Geneva, Switzerland. At recess, a new boy, much bigger than me, had been marking his turf on the playground. Shoving led to his spitting. As I spat back, we were both caught and sent to Mrs. Turner. After the stern talking to, she asked me to stay back. "Punch him in the face, yes. But don't spit, Naeem. That drops you to his level."

I am still surprised by her comment. Now I can see her: past the principal was the principle.

* * *

Ian McKay was my history teacher in eighth and ninth grade. Tall, bearded, and bespectacled, his demeanor was both intense and kind. He gave spellbinding lectures about slavery, about the origins of the

---

1. Course titles include: "Inequality in World Politics," "Theories of Exploitation," "Understanding Capitalism," "Foundations of Political Economy," "Politics of the Third World," "International Inequality," and "Capitalism and Ecology."

2. Course titles include: "Theories of International Relations," "Introduction to International Relations," "International Conflict," "Race and International Relations Theory," "Afghanistan and the Origins of Global Fury," "Religious Revolutions and Violence: Afghanistan, Iran, and the European Reformation," "Haiti and Bosnia Through Novels and Other Narratives," "Politics of South Asia," and "Cuba and Haiti."

3. Course titles include: "Ideas and Ideologies," "The U.S. and Genocide," "International Scholarly Conversation," "Writing and Criticism," "Liberalism and Marxism," "Agents, Structures, Action," "Shame, Apology, and Reparations," and "Love, Hate, and Sexual Desire Under Colonialism."

4. Course titles include: "Seeing 'War of the Worlds': Global Politics through Popular Films," "Worlds of Music," "Musical Meaning in a Global Context," "Global Musical Travel," "The Political Economy of African Diaspora Music," "Cultural Encounters," "Travel, Culture, and Modernity," and "Politics and Literature."

French Revolution, and on the World Wars. I don't remember the content well. The Lycée des Nations was a British school with a French name in a Swiss city. We were fewer than a dozen students in Mr. McKay's class. A classmate, Robert Fraser, came to school without a pretense about his studiousness. He partied hard and enjoyed shocking us with his knowledge of sexual anatomy. In history class one day, he immediately fell asleep as Mr. McKay unraveled for us the triggering events of World War I. Mr. McKay ignored Robert for a few moments, but the rest of us felt the discomfort of this breach in etiquette. Finally, he turned to Siri Meyer and said, "Can you find Robert a pillow, please?" This moment stays with me, but I don't know why.

One day, out of the blue, McKay asked to see me. Perhaps he sensed my teenage turmoil.

My father's fight with his immediate boss had ruffled his pride enough to resign. We would be heading from Geneva to Islamabad in mid-year—the very year that I seemed to be coming into my own body and mind. Girls were interested in me, and I could influence the flow of play on the soccer field.

Mr. McKay sat me down and suddenly offered: "My nationalism is fierce. But I make a good internationalist *because* of my total commitment to Scotland." End of conversation.

I had no idea what he meant nor why he directed this comment to me. But somehow, a version of his words appeared as an epigram to my master's thesis: "I am a 6,000-year-old Pushtun, a thousand-year-old Muslim, and a twenty-seven-year-old Pakistani," a quote attributed to Khan Abdul Wali Khan, the great freedom fighter against British colonialism. As it turned out, Mr. McKay's words were my first formal lesson in dialectics; that the abstract and the concrete are one and the same. We never really know what sticks or why.

* * *

When I met Sue Lambe, I knew that, despite her name, she was what I call a "mixo"—of mixed heritage (European and Japanese). She wrote a paper about how, when she turned sixteen and her hair became curly, she suddenly received considerable attention from men. She recounted her experience of being harassed while working in a printing factory the

year between high school and college. A salesman who worked there
would press his whole body into the back of hers and smell her long hair.

She cut her hair to experiment with the power of her curls. Her action deterred the harasser, but she also lost the attention she sought
from others. As she mused, "When the curls weren't-a-poppin', the
boys-weren't-a-knockin'." When in college, she once again cut her
long locks, and her philosophy professor, a man who never missed an
opportunity to flash his chest hair, expressed his disappointment and
disapproval to the entire class.

I had my own experiences of sporting shoulder-length hair at the age
of fourteen when my family moved from Geneva to Rawalpindi. There,
I had to elude threats from those men who saw my hair and then two
beats later saw my mustache. I suffered their anger when their projections on my hair were undone by my face.

My parents quickly insisted on haircuts. My lost curls both weakened and strengthened my resolve. Weakened because I felt powerless
to confront my culture and strengthened in that I planned a beard.

Since reading Sue's work, I have been mulling the power of hair.
These days, Sue creatively deploys her hair's multiple meanings. She
writes, "As I get older, I see that all the hair types I can have (straight,
curly, wavy, colors, lengths) shift the projective device that I am. . . ."

* * *

Gordon Lindsay is one of the best educators I have known. As my
high school teacher and coach, he cultivated my budding musical tastes
by exposing me to Miles Davis' electric phase. He coaxed out of me
a long paper on four of D. H. Lawrence's novels. Above all, Gordon
demonstrated how to portray friendship without either using or losing
his authority, until one day when I took him for granted and he flashed
his anger. I was late for communications class—a space, I just realized
this moment, where he experimented with alternative pedagogies. One
day, he would ask us to pose as statues for the entire period; another
day, we went out of the compound to shovel dirt off the road after rain.
Our interaction with Pakistani laborers, whom the city government sent
for that task, didn't go well—they took our desire to help as an affront
to their work ethic. We played chess tournaments. We acted as DJs and

produced music shows. We did whatever came to Gordon's mind. It was free and loose and fun and serious.

I knew it was time for class, but my table tennis opponent was Danielle Baron, the only girl to play on the boys' basketball team. We were both "on," as indicated by the long rallies for every point. It was less a competition and more a dance for which I decided to forgo Gordon's class. But he found me and, red-faced, yelled at me to get into class.

It was the first time I'd felt Gordon's anger. He didn't stress attendance, but I had betrayed, if only momentarily, some part of his trust. Trust was his medium, and his anger lingers. Not in a bad way; I still adore this man. Perhaps because I sensed for the first time a teacher's desire, their need.

* * *

John Denison was my high school physics teacher in Islamabad. With his permission, I memorized the stars of the northern hemisphere instead of writing a term paper on a famous cosmologist. On a dusty but clear Islamabad night, I used his flashlight to show our class the constellations and the visible planets. My sense of orientation started with Mr. Denison.

He'd perfected a teaching posture that still keeps me awake. He played the bumbling, confused teacher. We had then to constantly correct him. This is how he enticed us to learn. Of course, we knew that he was playing a role, and yet, he was utterly convincing both as the organizer of the larger stage and as the forgetful dupe.

I have played at this myself, but only tangentially, when students make strong criticisms of me that I do not want to complicate or correct. I want them instead to see that criticism does not require an immediate response. My ego can take this hit, but not every day, and not as a vocation. I wonder how Mr. Denison did it.

* * *

Subbiah Kannappan was my Indian economics professor in the 1970s when I was an undergraduate at Michigan State University. I was enrolled in his development economics course. In his class, I was a quiet student; I barely had the nerve to raise my hand, much less make a comment. But he must have seen something in my written work because, at the end of the semester, he directed me to work with him in an independent study. I had to figure out what an independent study was.

The format for my study was what I feared the most: a semester of solitary reading followed by a term paper that counted for 100 percent of my grade. I dreaded the pressure of a singular paper, which is why I had not completed the third course in my philosophy sequence. The last of these classes required a single paper at the end—a deal-breaker for me. But what can you do when a professor chooses you?

My paper compared India's and China's development paths, and upon reading it, Professor Kannappan strongly suggested a second independent study, this time on the "New International Economic Order." But by the end of the semester, I had done no work. I confessed. He responded with flat affect, "You didn't do anything, so you didn't lose anything. I'll give you an incomplete." That is how I learned of incompletes—a temporal paradox if ever there was one. Years later, in my second graduate program at the University of Denver, I had one left even after I completed my dissertation.

Professor Kannappan was neither charismatic nor did he offer some creative radical pedagogy. We barely even interacted. But he picked me. And he shaped me.

* * *

It's December 2009, and I have returned to Pakistan, in part because my father is in an advanced stage of Parkinson's disease. Next to him sits Abdur Raheem, a tall, good-looking boy of seventeen who, during the day, attends to my father's needs and at night sleeps on the floor next to him. He is doing it for the money and for the food and shelter of this house, but he also happens to be a good caretaker; it seems to fill some need in him. Certainly, he is better at it than Sudir, for whom he has just taken over, but the job will eventually wear him out like it did Sudir.

Given our fraught relationship, my father knows I am trying to avoid conversation with him. He does not call me for his never-ending requests for juice, the cell phone that his stiffened fingers no longer allow him to use, the newspaper which he will not read, or for his daily demand that we prepare for a trip to his village, to Lahore, or to Singapore, trips we will never make.

When my father awakens, he does not know where he is. He may believe he is in Kuala Lumpur, or Lahore, or Karachi, or Gujranwalla. He will ask me to send him the driver and to help arrange for plans to take the family to Islamabad or Bawaray Kohna—his ancestral village—or somewhere else. My mother sometimes indulges him and pantomimes these arrangements. But I don't play. I usually spend ten minutes repeating: "Dad, you are in the house you built in 1972 in Islamabad. This is your only house. You live here and have lived here continuously since you and the family moved back from Kuala Lumpur in 1983. There is no question of you going on any trip either since that would require that you become strong enough to sit up, stand, and walk. Once you are strong again, we can talk about a trip. Otherwise, there is no point in this conversation."

His laughter mocks me. Clearly, I don't understand, he says. He will turn to others to arrange the trip. When I pressed him one morning on why he wants so badly to travel every morning, he said: "I don't know where to go from here." That I get. He doesn't understand, as none of us do, where death will take him. So, he might as well aim for a destination of his own choosing.

The second part of the cycle starts around 10:00 a.m., after Abdur Raheem feeds him breakfast. Now he settles into the mundane details of his life. He is desperate for conversation—there is not much to be had, he thinks, from Abdur Raheem. When all else fails, he will talk, even to me. I am last on his list because I stand up to his bullying. Twice in the last three weeks, he has severed our conversation because he could not navigate the choppy seas that I bring to our relationship. This mundane fact is worth mentioning because it has never happened before; my father has always had endless energy for winning in conversation. If grinding, pulverizing talk were like chess, he would be its grandmaster. As my brother, Noman, whose skill with chess first outdid my own in a matter of days and then quickly shone past my father's, once said, "With dad, you can never win."

To get to my bedroom, I walk past my father at least twenty times a day. He is torn about engaging me because of the tangible anger he knows I am ready to express. I am prepared with accusations about his treatment of servants, women, and children, his miserly madness, his simultaneous drive for control and attention, and his surgical skill in excising what is vital in his children. I do not stand down on these issues just because of his authority, his age, or his poor health. I am quite un-Pakistani in this way. On the other hand, we both sense that time is short. I hear in his words a need for an implicit confession, apology, and all that follows from his shattered hubris. I allow myself to be pulled in, perhaps because I think I might finally, in my fifties, be ready for the challenge. I have reason to believe that I may not see him again after this trip, and while I do not believe that our reconciliation can happen within a single lifetime, for some reason, I find myself present.

I sit in front of him, secure in the knowledge that I can get up and go run errands and do chores for my mother, or I can just walk away. This freedom is novel. Nevertheless, I sit as he requests. He lectures me on how important it is for us to have a family discussion, then moves to a higher level of abstraction avoiding the specific issues that lie before us. I anticipate his strategy. He wants to establish the rules of engagement since he knows that I will not assume a posture of automatic respect for his status as an elder. He lays them out: one must be allowed to speak without interruption even if it hurts; one must speak without negativity and accusation; one must speak from a sense of love and healing.

Of course, I experience his rules as a way to deprive me of my defenses and to undo my protective supports.

I have told myself many times in these last few days of my four-week visit that there is no point in expressing my anger with him. But as he speaks, my rolling eyes cannot sustain interest. I have heard this talk since sixth grade. The irony of lecturing me on the rules of conversation is totally lost on him.

I force myself to try a different approach. Clifford Brown, perhaps the greatest jazz trumpeter, when asked about how he improvises, said that he thinks about what he does *not* want to play. He does not want to play what he has played before. He tarries with the negative.

I think of Clifford and interrupt, "Dad, I have ample experience with you lecturing me but no memory of you listening to me. So now, when you lecture, I don't listen."

No effect. Over and over, he tells me how to live, how to listen, how to speak, how to access my deeper desires.

I try a different tactic. "Why do you keep telling me things that I already know and have spent my life thinking about or things that you know I disagree with?" This stops his tape but only for a moment. Soon the tape rolls on. I interrupt again. "Dad, dad, every time that you start talking about how we should create a dialogue, you end up lecturing me."

He stops.

But then he moves to a completely new strategy—unheard of in my life with him. He echoes back to me what I have said: "You are saying that my attempts at dialogue end up as monologues."

"Yes," I say in amazed disbelief.

There is a pause, between life and death perhaps. "Let me think about why I do that," he says.

I laugh an adult's laugh and chide him, "Self-reflection, Dad. That's a good thing."

After some moments, he astonishes me again. "I turn dialogue into monologue, and the reason I do this is because I think I am superior."

I cannot believe my ears. "Yes, yes," I say. His self-reflection begets mine: "I don't blame you for that though, this is what teachers and parents do." I want to suggest the structured nature of turning dialogue into monologue. He wants to think more about this pattern.

He offers a poem in Urdu that he interprets for me. The point of the poem is this: he has pursued knowledge (and the status and rewards that come with some forms of knowledge) at the costs of all else, especially matters of the heart. This has been the central mistake of his life. He did not understand that there is only one tangible wealth—that which comes in relationships with others.

Even more than the content, I am excited by his form. I say, "Instead of lecturing, you are offering me a confession. This moves me."

My joy is short-lived. He's back into lecturing—this time on how I can live my life with love and harmony. Again, I think of Clifford. "Can I tell you a story, Dad?" I don't wait for assent. "When I was in the hospital, I was attended to by a cardiologist who was 150 pounds overweight. I wondered why I should be doctored by someone who cannot manage his own health."

He doesn't make the connection. I explain:

"You've just confessed that you lived a life based on a mistake. So, why should I listen to your advice?"

"Good point. I will need to think about that." Then silence.

We had bypassed the competition that had always characterized our interactions to work together for something else. It was my father's last gift to me.

At lunch, I give my sister a report on this moment. She pronounces it a miracle: "I never got anything like that from him in my whole life." It is the virtue of his diminished memory.[5]

* * *

The more we learn about the world, the more we might agree that "knowledge is power." This aphorism suggests that we can make the world just and beautiful through knowledge.

But "knowledge is power" contains ominous overtones. It also means that the powerful acquire knowledge to do *their* bidding. Through knowledge, we produce justice and beauty but also inequality and brutality. As knowledge enters us, it also turns us towards its dark side. In embracing knowledge, we may find ourselves being controlled by its power.

Acknowledging this contradiction didn't come easily to me. It went against everything I hoped for. I wanted to go to school, get many degrees, and become a professor because I thought schools, teachers, and knowledge were all on the side of goodness and justice. Then, some thirty years ago, I read three books back to back: Edward Said's *Orientalism*, Tzvetan Todorov's *The Conquest of America*, and Ashis Nandy's *The Intimate Enemy*. Their unmistakable conclusion left me shaken: the powerful use knowledge to dominate, to subjugate, and to terrorize. *Our educational institutions function as the brain of the death star.* A career in education is a career in domination. I don't know if I will ever recover from this claim, but I cannot deny it.

After nearly forty-eight years in higher education—thirty-five of them as a teacher—I have finally allowed myself to confront *this* question: "Could it be that no one wants to learn?" No one wants to learn because learning threatens to dissolve nations, break families, wreck

---

5. I am grateful to Cory Brown for this line.

friendships, and shatter the wholesomeness of the self.[6] Could this be the cause of my teaching failures?

* * *

I discovered my commitment to criticism when I was invited to give a talk on my "spiritual journey" at a church in Corning, New York. I started with Marx.

Marx's critique of capitalism parallels his critique of religion. Like many before him, he believes that humans make God an idol to which they submit, to which they give up their power. He calls it alienation.

Marx's reference to religion as the "opiate of the masses" is well known. But I didn't know the full quote: "Religion is the sigh of the oppressed creature, the heart of a heartless world, and the soul of soulless conditions. It is the opium of the people."[7] Marx wants to bring our attention to why this sigh—the "sigh of the oppressed"—is necessary.

Doubt, death, and mortality require us to give our temporary stay here meaning. Sometimes, I ask my students to recall the Ten Commandments. As they do so, I write them on the board. Standing back from the board, I say: "The desire to do the opposite of those Commandments is what worries the Commandment makers. Desire makes those Commandments necessary, no? The Commandments direct us to check and deny our desire." Sometimes I mention that the Lacanians believe that it is the Commandments' prohibitions that produce desire. Intensifying the ban creates a parallel attraction to what the ban is meant to prevent.

Such a paradox makes it easy for me to reject the angry or compassionate anthropomorphic white male God with a white beard and white hair—Gandalf the White. I reject, too, that God interferes in human life. I came to this when co-teaching a course with my biology department colleague, Susan Swensen Witherup. This means no miracles for me, even if I often pray for them. Nevertheless, I do accept the mystery and

---

6. Elizabeth Dauphinee responds: "Jesus says, 'I have not come to make peace, but to turn son against father and daughter against mother. . . .' Elsewhere, he says, 'No one can come with me unless he hates his family, and is willing to disavow his life.' Elsewhere, he says to a man who asks him to wait while he buries his father: 'Leave the dead to bury the dead.'"

7. Marx, Karl. (1976). "Introduction to a Contribution to the Critique of Hegel's Philosophy of Right," in Collected Works, vol. 3. New York: International Publishers.

awe of the natural and social world. My knees buckle in the presence of an alpine tundra, my heart melts at the sight of a knowing smile, and I am overcome by the glimpse of a shooting star. If God is anything, then God is immanent within the mundane processes of everyday life.

But my penchant for the immanent does not mean that there is no room for the transcendent.

When I listen to the grandmaster of the piano Chucho Valdes play with his quartet, I am moved to tears. Chucho is a medium who brings the transcendent gods halfway down to us while elevating us with his music. He transports us to that contact zone. Such euphoria is the closest thing I can describe to a religious experience. The classical vocals of South Asia and the ripping/healing tenor sax of Pharaoh Sanders produce the same effect on me.

So there are no churches, synagogues, mosques, or temples for me. Instead, I make my pilgrimages to hear these musical prophets. These teachers have given my life some depth, and they have done so without words.

Despite what you may read in the news, contemporary Pakistan is not wholly an austere place—there is an enjoyment of life there that puts Western suburbs to a gray shame. Nevertheless, one of the ideals in Pakistan is to memorize the Quran. My sister, fifteen years my junior and born in Geneva, has done so. Moreover, she can translate the Arabic she reads into the Urdu and English she speaks.

My mother received the highest education her village could offer a young girl in the 1940s, fifth grade, but she was born into a scholarly and religious family. Her grandfather was Shia, and her father became Sunni after his travels to the Deoband, a religious university in current-day India. She memorized the Quran, and she knows what it means. Although she gives weekly lectures at various venues in Islamabad, I only learned of her teaching a few years ago.

My father, too, was a kind of religious leader in his village. He once led Friday prayers, I am told. Eventually, however, he converted to science and devoted his life to consolidating the social sciences in Pakistan. Between my father and mother, there was a kind of war that lasted a lifetime. He accepted that she dreamed the future while he teased her about her belief in angels. She tolerated his condescension but considered him a lost soul.

I live in the overlap of science and the mystical traditions of religions. I take it for granted that science is a system of belief, that it requires leaps of faith, and, therefore, that we can think of it as a kind of spirituality.

I am devoted to the precision that science brings. If I cannot be precise about why I believe something, how I am moved by something, or why I make something, then I have betrayed the spirit of what it means to be a human.

However, precision for its own sake is a fetish. Precision's purpose is to serve the larger story that doubt, death, and mortality impel us to construct.

Above all, I believe in criticism, in the positive power of the negative. I reject peaceful love. Peace is the name given to a conquered desolation; love is the name given to the habits with which we have made peace. The first part of this sentence describes my father's limitations; the second is my mother's.

But what I *can* get behind is critical love—the idea that whatever we are, we are not just that. There is no assumption that cannot be undone, and in that undone negative space, there is something we can reap.

* * *

Hope betrays us. It makes us blink in the face of truth. It lulls us towards a nostalgia for innocence. Hope is the betrayer, the liar, the thorn in the paw of our courage. Such hope forces us to keep an eye on the fuel gauge and not on the road. Crushed hope, on the other hand, is a viable resource. The only viable resource.

CHAPTER 3

Apprenticeship

Graduate School and Junior Faculty Trials

In 1988, I was thirty-two with a freshly minted PhD in international studies and a tenure-track job at Syracuse University. I requested a meeting with the chair of my department and asked him why professors must publish their work: "I understand why I teach, research, and write. But what's the point of publishing?"

"To build an archive," he said.

I acknowledged his response, but it left me no more enlightened. Writing for an abstract and anonymous reader overwhelmed me because I could not imagine saying something meaningful and enduring. Later, I realized that I needed to write to friends and colleagues, and they to me, so that the archive could be something living we created between us.

* * *

James Caporaso was an internationally recognized scholar when I was working with him as a graduate student. At the time, I was not aware that schools were scheming to steal him from the University of Denver. Remarkably, the hardest-working man in academia lives a balanced life. His passions include fly fishing, gourmet cooking, and an enduring love of athletics. Every so often, he played basketball with us, but his sport of preference was handball, for which he donned special gloves.

The handball court was deep in the bowels of the gym, past the squash courts and adjacent to a musty, poorly ventilated, dark space that passed for a weight room. I was there three times a week to tighten my shoulder joints and to fight the approaching tragedy of my thirtieth birthday. While working on my dissertation, which, as many of us know, is really shuffling through the reasons we are not working on our dissertation, I announced to everyone who would listen that my first love was still perfecting my beautiful jump shot.[1] I cared not at all about winning lunch-time basketball games. I just wanted to outrun everyone and swish the nets. If my shot was on point, the euphoria could sustain me for weeks.

As I lifted weights and stretched endlessly, Jim would sometimes peek in, maybe do some lifting, and then get on with his handball game. One day in May, he entered and gave me an extended look as if he were assessing a possibility.

"You have a minute?" he asked.

I walked out to the hallway thinking, *Anything for you, Jim.*

"My colleagues at CU (University of Colorado) are looking for someone to teach courses in IR (International Relations). Think you could do that?"

I freeze into stillness, during emergencies, when confronted with severe criticism and in moments of great thrill. At first, this behavior was involuntary. Now that age has made this response no longer necessary, I take it on willingly.[2] It gives me time to hear. I slow down.

"Yes, I can," I finally said. A lie.

But I had the summer to read, prepare the courses, and turn that lie into truth. There was a bonus: the job would defer the great battle with that monster called the dissertation. I would escape via jump shots and jobs.

In mid-summer, I walked to Jim's office, the largest on the third floor of Ben M. Cherrington Hall with a huge wall of windows facing east towards the Iliff School of Theology where Paulo Freire had headlined an event. According to lore, Freire opened each presentation with

---

1. I often repeated the famous Otis Birdsong quote: "Three things you can count on: death, taxes, and my jumper."

2. "As academics are trained for the warfare of ideas and may be committed to the various truths of the profession, they may have no sympathy for ambivalence and non-defensive thought. . . . The idealization of professional mastery, to the extent it demands full conviction and vilifies hesitation, disorientation, and ambivalent silence, idealizes the desire not to know. The life of reason is thus undermined by the very professionalism that ostensibly supports it." Alcorn, Marshall. (2013). *Resistance to Learning* (New York: Palgrave Macmillan), p. 130.

two words, "Any questions?" forgoing all prepared notes for immediate direct dialogue. Turned out, he presented for five minutes before he turned to the needs of the audience. It was a memorable performance. Half a decade later, I would read two of his books[3] that my student Mary Markowicz threw on my lap as a remedy to my despondence at the failure of one of my teaching experiments. Then Freire's words revitalized me.

When my turn came at his office hours, I asked Jim for his "Introduction to International Relations" syllabi. He walked the fifteen steps from his desk to his filing cabinet as I took in the view outside his window. He searched for a bit, pulled out a syllabus, and walked towards me. Then in mid-step, he stopped, returned the papers to his file, and announced: "No. You'll develop your own take."

I walked away unable to fathom his subtleties. It wasn't the first time he confused me.

Eventually, I developed the course around the work of Hedley Bull and Richard Mansbach, Yale Ferguson, and Donald Lampert, a few of the only works that gave me a historical sense of International Relations.[4] Still, I wasn't sure that this is what my employers wanted. I called Mike Ward, Jim's friend and colleague, requesting context: What did the department need? What were the students like? To what kinds of reading might they respond well? He interrupted: "I've hired you so I don't have to think about these things."

Today, thirty-seven years later, I have just been speaking to a recent hire who asked me the same questions about her first semester of teaching at Ithaca College. I recounted to her my Mike Ward story.

Like her, I was on my own. Well, not quite. Always present is the invisible universal inquisitor for whom we leave a trail of damning evidence. I always kept an eye on the classroom door, thinking that someone in a tweed jacket and dark glasses would invade my classroom and bust me for my irresponsible teaching decisions. Without that inquisitor, I might just have taught novels from the start.

* * *

3. *Pedagogy of the Oppressed* and, with Ira Shor, *Pedagogy for Liberation.*
4. Hedley Bull, *The Anarchical Society,* 1977; Bull and Watson, *The Expansion of International Society,* 1984; and Mansbach, Ferguson, and Lampert, *The Web of World Politics,* 1976.

Some twenty years ago, at an International Studies Association conference, Justin Rosenberg was demolishing Anthony Giddens' latest ideas. I bristled because of my fidelity to Giddens' older work. As an undergraduate, I had read his *Capitalism and Modern Social Theory* (1971) and had recently re-read his three books on structuration.

Outraged, I suggested that Justin might do well to respect a theorist who had done so much to update dialectics. He seemed a bit taken aback.

In retrospect, my anger emerged not so much from the affront to Giddens but from what Justin's critique meant for my memory of James McKee, the understated sociology professor who opened for me the worlds of Durkheim, Marx, and Weber. Justin's argument challenged my loyalty to McKee.

* * *

My student, Adin Michelen, and I were probing stories with the class about our greatest fears. Mine are heights and public speaking. Adin talked about his own fear of heights. "I cannot get near the edge . . ." he started to say when I interrupted to finish his thought, "Because you are afraid you might slip and fall." "No, no, no . . ." he corrected, "because I'm afraid I might jump off."

I had never allowed myself to see that this was what I might be thinking.

* * *

It is spring 1986. I am a graduate student teaching my first class at the University of Denver. My cohort has been offered classes, and I am the last to be considered for a spot. None of my graduate school buddies had asked me to present a guest lecture. They may have guessed at the disarray I might cause.

I put in thirty hours a week on the course to the neglect of my dissertation. I give up some of my lunch-hour pick-up basketball games. At the end of the course, I think I have done well, but three of the nine evaluations find the course mediocre; another three reveal that the course was a miserable failure. "But why?" I ask as I clutch the evaluations. How does sincere, hard, good work produce failure? Couldn't they see my effort? What I created for them? Why didn't they provide hints of their unhappiness?

For days and weeks, I cannot be consoled. I cry openly. My partner wonders what she has gotten herself into; the word "dissertation" is already banned from the house and now *this* misery.

I take my disbelief and despondency to three of my mentors. Create distance, they suggest. I replace the blue jeans and backpack with ties and a briefcase. I no longer sit on the table. Distance, I discover, can be a means to intimacy.[5]

* * *

It's fall 1986, and I have three courses at the University of Colorado in Boulder. I have spent the summer reading utterly lifeless textbooks. I am teaching five days a week; each day includes a three-hour commute on six buses. But I know I am fortunate to land this job.

In my tweed jacket and beige tie, I arrive forty minutes early for my first class. I look to the west at the Flatirons and think of how many times I have hiked there, even though heights and public speaking are my two great fears. I remain unconvinced that in forty minutes a voice will emerge from me. Then again, the mountains are no less daunting.

I am in the class now with 120 eager students. I open my mouth, and for a few seconds, there is nothing. I have no backup plan. Then I hear my voice as it climbs up towards the students. It is a miracle.

Weeks have gone by, and I am covering, one by one, the various schools of international relations theory. I have reams of lecture notes on yellow notepad paper. I am beginning to relax, make jokes, and tell stories. They seem to be responding to the material and to me. But I am still injured and wary from my prior experience.

I get to the section on game theory. Even today, I cannot abide game theory or what we might call methodological economism. It reduces all human motivations to *a*cultural and *a*historical rationalities. I think of it as a kind of epistemological death star, which, with laser precision, finds and obliterates all non-economic social relations, the very relations that support the economy. Back then, I couldn't have expressed

---

5. I take this to be modernity's great contribution to our understanding of the world.

all this. A summary rejection of game theory is all I had. I take a deep breath, thinking that despite my misgivings, I owe this to them and to the profession.

Twenty minutes into the second day of game theory, I look up to see their vacant eyes. Perhaps they sense that I myself am not really there. I stop. I stumble. I delay, and then I confess: "You know I hate game theory. I really think it's bullshit, and I don't know why I am even presenting it." Several of them give me the side-eye. Minutes go by as I battle with myself. I'm in a pivotal moment of my teaching career. "To hell with it," I say, "no more game theory." Their collective relief embraces me, but I am flooded with anxiety. I cannot shake the shadow of the academic police, who I imagine are waiting to call me out.

* * *

I'm in the second semester of my teaching career. Some way into the semester, I work myself into a gently escalating emotional pitch, building a solo as jazz greats Dexter Gordon or Coleman Hawkins might do. But my voice breaks when I reach the crescendo, and I am overblowing as Archie Shepp and Roscoe Mitchell might do. I deliver a witty and disdainful jab at some abstract villain—state bureaucrats, probably. However, it's not my meaning but the texture of my sound that stays with the students. As I express the scream caught in my throat, the hundred or so students burst into spontaneous applause.

Random occurrence, I think, like a hailstorm. I give it no more thought.

It happens again the following semester. It's a different stage and new audience but the same performance and ovation. I lower my head, seething and glaring at my feet. It's easy to get used to and, therefore, dangerous. I am determined to never again let this happen.[6]

* * *

The next semester I had a lighter load; 120 students, but only one class. I carried over my anger at my apparent success with students.

---

6. Elizabeth Dauphinee responds: "You take something away from those of us in the theatre who witness this kind of event and experience it as a catharsis. It is not only or always about ease or power. Sometimes it is about deep admiration, amazement, love. And applause is all they have in the landscape of a lecture hall." My response: the moment felt dangerous from the premonition of what I might become if I started to feed on it.

I had been too easy, too populist. I appeared now in the persona of the sarcastic professor who treats students as fools who don't do the readings, don't take notes, and waste their wealthy Western education. Jibes fly out from me at no particular target.

Five weeks into the course, I received an envelope from one of the students who sat in the front. She was short, wearing glasses, and exuding gravitas. I wished I had saved that four-page typed memo.

In it, she wrote: "There are five of us in the front who do the readings, never miss class, take good notes, and wish to learn. Stop your bitching and teach." I read that letter twenty times.

* * *

Another student, James Voss, wanted to become a fighter pilot. He seemed fit for the role: part student, part wonder-boy superhero. His crew cut and military ambitions had me reluctant to engage with him fully. Back in 1986, I was still developing my stance toward students whose politics I might oppose. Then one day, he walked in with his copy of Ngũgĩ wa Thiong'o's *Petals of Blood* and teased, "Aren't you tired of Achebe's *Things Fall Apart*? I know I am. Here, try this instead." My first lesson in the subterfuge of identity.

* * *

My spouse, Sorayya Khan, and I move to Syracuse. Leaving Denver's 320 days of sunshine for a perennially cloudy city simmering in rust is disheartening. I am teaching two sections of a graduate course on International Relations theory—thirty students per section. The morning class always goes well. But the afternoon section responds to my thirty-minute presentations with silence.

I fail on the first day when a Palestinian student wonders what my world of theory can say to his experience of dispossession. "Absolutely nothing!" My exasperation oozes out of me, crying, "This is my first semester of teaching graduate theory, and you are throwing the reality of Palestine at me! Please, give me a fucking break." I say none of that to him, of course. But he and the class make perfect sense of my glares, my silence, and my choked fury. They understand that the theoretical professionalism I require to advance my career outweighs their practical urgency. Perhaps this is why they punish me with their silence for the rest of the semester.[7]

My frustration with them moves me into crisis mode. I read Henry Kariel's provocative essay, "Becoming Political." Kariel's writing strategy slows all events so that we can see their process of becoming. Silence, too, he treats as a potentially productive ally. I try his methods. I accede to their quietness. I strain my ears to distinguish their different textures.

Discussion ensues because I outlast them with my new techniques, but I lack something. Everything is forced. I never think of this class without hating it.

* * *

It is spring of 1991, and I am teaching Politics of South Asia at Syracuse University. Throughout graduate school, I have assiduously avoided *all* courses that might credential me as a South Asian specialist, while proudly wearing my "theory" qualifications. Yet, here I am, pinned as the native informant.

The Gulf War is obliterating my unexamined assumptions about scholarship. Do I incorporate the war into my class? Do I proclaim my partisanship? What is my duty here? The war will serve as a permanent wedge and a sledgehammer in my relationship with one of my mentors. We probably agreed on the wrongness of the war. In contention was the role of the academic.

Frustration envelopes me; I cannot sort out my responsibilities, and this triggers my tantrum at the fifty or so students. I don't remember what I said. But I replay the scene upon returning to my office. I was certain that I had lost them, that I had been irresponsible, that I was a terrible teacher, and that they would strike back in their evaluations. At the end of the semester, as I read their assessments, I noted that they mentioned that day as pivotal to the course. Here is the surprise: they did not experience my frustration as wholly negative. I called in a couple of them to help me understand. They said, "We knew then you had something at stake."

---

7. Laura McNeal responds: "It seems possible to me that they were simply being silent because they were afraid of the Palestinian's [student's] gargantuan question. Instead of being a class, it became a geopolitical event, one in which they didn't know how to act."

This class's bounty provides a second story. I received a midterm paper making the argument that if the British had paid more attention to India's culture and improved their communication skills, they would have been able to sustain their empire. The student concludes that the British might have prolonged their empire had they learned more about Indian culture and local modes of communication.

In retrospect, I see now that she had anticipated the US military's "Human Terrain System" strategy of imperial conquest in Iraq and Afghanistan. But back then, I was in no humor to play. I slapped down an "F."

Doing so unsettled me. I walked around the building a few times trying to think of what I might say in my comments. Grades without comments are never a possibility.

Days later, I cross out the grade. How can I fail a sincere effort? What can I do? It finally comes to me—build the house on the rift, even though this language would not be available to me for decades. I ask her to read the paper in class, betting that her classmates will provide the well-thought-out critique that I cannot summon without exploding.

To my horror, all but five of the students sway to her rhythm. These remaining five read the room and, like me, were either unwilling or unable to express their anger. Renouncing academia was never far from my mind in those days. I walk away stumped, defeated. What use am I if I cannot get them to see their receptiveness to colonialism?

Michael Walzer, a famed scholar who some claim to have single-handedly invented "just war theory," is the keynote speaker at the Northeast International Studies annual conference in Philadelphia. The organizers, no doubt, beamed at hosting a famed scholar who also whispered advice in the halls of absolute power. I, too, am there to hear what a "Michael Walzer" might sound like. The well-lit and historically rich ballroom is full of eager graduate students and junior faculty ready to add to their list of "famous scholars I have seen." I am outraged as I put together what I hear: Walzer believes that the US invasion of Iraq is ethically indefensible, but he nevertheless wants to build an argument for an ethical *occupation* of Iraq. He takes his time to spin his web in a space so secure that his spectators happily allow him a separation between invasion and occupation. The room glows, and his gentle strokes have them purring. All but two of us. My colleague from Nigeria is the first to ask a question, and the hostility in her tone announces that she, at least, has not been duped.

The reason I could contain my fury, wait for my turn, and then ask my question with detached professional demeanor is because I recognize that Walzer's argument reflects the student paper from my South Asia course. As my heart pounds, I ask: "How does your argument differ from a defense of colonialism?" He parses words, mixes themes, and loses us all in a tortured monologue. Our interventions have, of course, no effect on the seduction at play. Walzer receives a standing ovation, during which no one notices that my Nigerian colleague and I sit with our jaws clenched.

Subsequently, I note a shift in my posture. I discover that the heroes of our profession are invested in empire, and I feel betrayed. Eventually, I arrive at a darker structural conclusion. Walzer and I are not so different. We both belong to a profession whose purpose is to support and excuse empire. Dissenting postures, like mine, do not matter much. We are all inside the belly of the beast because there is no outside.

* * *

I recall a formative meeting with my department chair when I was a junior faculty member at Syracuse University. He meant to support my career with this advice: I should aim to publish at only the top journals and presses in my field, and I should enhance my status as a scholar by downplaying my budding reputation as a good teacher. "We all like to do things we are good at, and this habit gets in the way of doing the important things," he said. Publishing was what was important.

Excellence in teaching was never my goal. Rather, I strove to develop student interest in international inequality. Behind this objective were a set of hidden assumptions. I probably wanted them to acknowledge their role in the perpetuation of international inequality, to feel complicit in it, and to work toward dismantling it.[8] But I began to realize that most of my students regarded colonial history as generally benign. The fissure between my efforts and my results was wide and deep.[9]

---

8. L. S. Stavrianos' *Global Rift: The Third World Comes of Age* (1981) is the one text that has remained a constant in my three-decade career. I suspect this means something.

9. ". . . what the teacher 'teaches' and what the student 'learns' will always be different, even radically so. But it is precisely the role of pedagogies and theories of pedagogies to cover over this radical split and impute to the pedagogy a certain cause-and-effect relation." Rickert, Thomas. (2007). *Acts of Enjoyment* (Pittsburgh: University of Pittsburgh Press), p. 112.

To reduce this gap, I restructured my teaching in three ways. First, I stopped expecting students to identify with my theoretical interests. Instead, I vowed to meet them at their own desires. I gleaned their motivations, deduced their thought process, and searched for the overlaps between our needs. Second, I had to change the *form* of my communication. Lecturing gave way to discussion, and discussion was peppered with Socratic interrogation within the classroom and during office hours. Third, it occurred to me that I could subject my teaching methods to critical examination. I researched the dynamics and history of teaching. I began to reorganize my classrooms with a sense of theoretically informed experimentation while working through Paulo Freire, Henry Kariel, and then, later, Marshall Alcorn and Thomas Rickert.

My current practice emerges from a set of foundational questions: Are teaching and learning really possible? If learning separates students from their former identity, how can they afford it? Even then, if some students wish to be separated from their former identities, then isn't my teacherly presence superfluous? What exactly is my role?

* * *

Team teaching is treacherous, but I won't tell you to avoid it.

In solo teaching, you get weeks to unfold your method, secure in the knowledge that the end-of-semester assessments may or may not be pivotal to your income stream. In team teaching, judgment is a drone strike. It is immediate and decisive.

At Syracuse, either I was oblivious to the warnings provided by coming thunder, or I sought subconsciously to be washed away by the storm that blew me sixty miles south to Ithaca. Of course, my paucity of publications played a role in my drama. Still, I cemented my reputation as "impossible" during a collective project.

In the early 1990s, a somewhat anonymized right-wing group funded a project with the goal of producing a unifying or capstone experience for students in higher education. It was seen as a solution to the problem of an atomized student body working under a scattered curriculum taught by professors devoted to the relativism of values.

Presto: "Contemporary Developments in International Political Economy" ensued, which was a course taught by nine professors, each with their own small section. The three remaining professors were part of the writing program who rotated through all the sections. There was also a weekly meeting in a large hall where the professors would take turns lecturing to the entire collection.

John Baker designed the course, selected the faculty, and convened us. He was happy to recruit me and the two other "faculty of color," as we might say, for the lack of a better term. I was never sure how much color we brought to the proceedings outside of the complex denotations delivered by our bodies. Whiteness ruled the proceedings, like greyness enfolds the Syracuse sky. But this I could not articulate at the time; I just knew that something was wrong in how our bodies were deployed, and my body was driven to express that something.

What was wrong? An icy, pedagogical thinness that could not but lead to tumbles, bruises, accusations, and, eventually, reprimands, apologies, and my ejection.

A few of the senior faculty members were internationally renowned scholars on top of which they had garnered teaching awards. It was impressive because teaching was something they did as a point of pride and as an aside from their scholarship. Their inquisitiveness, however, was confined to research. They did not imagine that their teaching, too, could fire their curiosity at its center. Nor did they share with their students what they were trying to learn. In short, they were unconscious to the possibility of theorizing their teaching. Teaching was something they did *to* students, not *with* them. Students were a means to accomplish the job of conveying information, not co-learners with whom one could expose a puzzle, a curiosity, or a vexation at the core of one's being. They reminded me of my father.

My alienation from the project sedimented when we were asked to wear alternative theoretical "hats" representing different paradigms for understanding political economy: "realism," "economic nationalism," and "international idealism." As we donned different hats, we were meant to demonstrate to the students how each paradigm apprehended some empirical reality, for example, the economic policies of the United States versus those of Germany and Japan.

My passion for highlighting the structural plight of the Third World, for example, had to be checked at the door. Until, that is, I placed the proper "structural Marxist" hat on my head. Then I could speak but only in the insipid tones of a professor, not as an advocate.

The result was that we hid from the student's view our political differences, our different pedagogies, and our different understanding of a university's mission. In effect, we were engaged in a smoothing operation that sutured these differences and effaced the deepest structural rift: the one between professors and students.[10] We were playing the game of teaching, and we were asking students to play along. They were happy to do so because they had been socialized to believe that learning means telling teachers what they want to hear. As I often say to students, "We pretend to teach; you pretend to learn."

I did not consider an iota of this at the time. I just knew that I was being asked to contain something vital in me. So, I struck back by improvising instead of playing by the script and by exposing as many of the rifts as I could. Maybe team teaching is dangerous because I enjoy danger.

In the large lecture, I produced an improvisation that was later remembered by my enunciating this question: "Are we 'Third Worlders' [my term for 'persons of color'] not domesticated animals in an academic zoo?" My two colleagues "of color" did not take well to my interpellation of them. Each angrily responded to my question with a fervor usually unseen in classrooms. One of them, from Somalia, required a written apology from me. As a concession to the Somali professor, John took it upon himself to apologize for what I said and for his "failure of leadership" in not immediately calling me out to the entire class.

At the time, I had no idea of the forces I had unleashed. But I will come to that shortly. First, I want to note something that occurs to me only because of this writing. What was missing and what I wanted was suddenly present: the biography of the teachers, our stakes in this mission, our substantive and pedagogical splits. We had moved from playing a game of "hats" to the reality of heated investments. I had forced them to become visible. No wonder their resentment. How could I have missed it?

---

10. "There exists a fundamental antagonism between teacher and student that cannot be avoided or dissipated. . . . Pedagogy is the process that organizes itself around this impasse, a dichotomy that exists in the material situation of the classroom." Rickert, *Acts of Enjoyment*, 2007, p. 118.

The end-of-the-semester celebration was at Lemon Grass, a new Thai restaurant, still then at its location at a strip mall in Mattydale. With dessert arriving, and my false sense that I had been forgiven, Alan White, the highest-ranking of us, turned to me: "You seem to think that what we did was a waste of time." He was not asking me a question. He was triggering what I recall as an ambush. The writing faculty remained quiet, but the rest of them followed White's lead and expressed their disgust at my audacity and betrayal. I absorbed their words by focusing on my breathing.

It's true, I provoked them, and I had coming what they delivered. In retrospect, I am not sure what I would have wanted from them instead as we sat at that dinner table. Perhaps someone to laugh and say, "You are young, foolish, and risk-prone. It will take you some time to harness your raw abilities." Perhaps all I needed then was a hint, that yes, teaching could be a kind of co-presence and someone to make me feel a bit less alone.

Please don't misunderstand; I'm not talking about loneliness. I mean aloneness, a sense that one's labor is performed absent an echo from others. Is this not the great barrier to creativity? That, for the absence of some resonance, one gives up before one begins.

* * *

To John's great credit, he did not give up on me. That would take a second round with another team of teachers whose exasperation with me finally tied John's hands and led to my expulsion from all future team teaching at Syracuse.

The plan for the second version of the course differed in that the team (this time including graduates and undergraduate students) met once weekly to become familiar with each other, prepare a strategy, and produce a syllabus. We started by sharing readings, but it quickly became apparent that we were sharing parts of ourselves.

Peggy Simon had us read *Child of the Dark: The Diary of Carolina Maria De Jesus* (1963), which she successfully used in her courses. The book purports to be the diary of a woman with "two years of schooling" who lives in a Brazilian favela with her three children. The story showcases her stark poverty and the daily grind of her miserable existence. Reading it, I noted that there was no evidence that this woman ever laughed, played, or felt any joy. The book was edited by a journalist, Audalio Dantas, and it was unclear to me whether the diary selections reflected the author's vision of her life or the editor's desire to call attention to poverty and to poverty alone. Regardless, the book did not capture the fuller life of those with little means.

Our group did not receive this book with the adulation that Professor Simon expected. Indeed, she seemed shocked that Paul Hilton, an undergraduate on the team, offered criticism. But it was my amplification of Paul's criticisms that grated on her. Before long, I was called into the office of the Assistant Dean and given the terms for my continuation on the team: a written apology to Professor Simon followed by its delivery in her office. I confused the Dean. He kept asking me, "Why do you keep acting like you are a minority hire?" By which he meant that there was no need for me to feel the pressure of representing a segment of the population.

I wrote the apology, but my presentation was vociferously rejected by Professor Simon. When I look back, I demeaned myself for groveling, for wanting to hang on. "You should have held on to your principles," I admonish my younger self.

Which principles? That the academy was a space in which we expressed public criticism, an institution that appraised and welcomed, above all, the ideas themselves. I wavered between the innocence of full belief and the not-quite-visible agenda of skewering the institution with its own standards. Courage is sometimes a unicorn on the horizon, an illusion that appears tangible. I vacillated between the extremes of worrying that they were on to me, that they realized they had made a poor hire when they discovered how hard I had to work. And, on the other hand, that they had become aware of my longing to meet people who were half as smart as my graduate school colleagues and mentors. No doubt Professor Simon could sense the latter half of my split self.

Fred Calvin, another faculty team member, did me in with his ultimatum that the price of his continued presence was dropping me from the team.

Calvin flew back and forth between Syracuse and Washington, DC, where he consulted for the World Bank. His selected reading for our team was a ten-page article on development economics. John and I were likely the only two acquainted with the jargon.

Calvin became angry and then punishing when all nine of us failed to respond to his article. I had vowed not to go first, and John was practicing good skills by leading from behind. Calvin concluded that none of us had toiled hard enough. He started shaming us for our lack of industry. Finally, I intervened by addressing myself to the team and not to Calvin: "All the assumptions are in the first two paragraphs. The rest of the piece is merely an application of those assumptions. If we spend our energy on the first paragraph, we will have read the piece."

I have read Adam Smith's *Wealth of Nations* many times, but there are perhaps only forty of its pages on which I have focused. I have read Marx's *Capital* (volume 1) so many times that I have had to purchase multiple copies. Most of my current sabbatical was spent on reading books that would teach me to read this book. These books are as much about *Capital* as they are about how to read. Once we recognize that there are many, many theories of reading, we spend the rest of our lives learning to read.

Of course, the entire team had read every word of Calvin's offering; he didn't really doubt that. But we all understood that to read something means more than to scan all the words. What is that "something more"? For Calvin, we needed to decipher the jargon and internalize the argument. For me, that day, it meant finding and querying the hidden ground on which the argument was based. What it means for me *today* is uncovering how the structure of an argument produces logical flows, contradictions, and silences. See what I mean? I am still working through various theories of reading.

You can guess that our economist colleague had not perhaps entertained the possibility that each of his team came to a text with a well-practiced but different theory of reading. Nor could we articulate to him how we each had read. To the World Bank-credentialed economics professor, our silence meant that we were uninformed. He likely saw my failed attempt to translate as a turn to the relativism of values. If so, I now understand his need to evict me. Better to think of his colleagues as uninterested and lazy than to see himself as just one among many interpreters of a text, as one native among other natives. Economists cannot abide anthropologists.

* * *

Mark Rupert and I were partners for many years at Syracuse University. He preceded me by a year, and he doubtless played a role in my hiring. We commiserated as only those can who are highly stressed junior faculty in a department of seniors to whom the tenure process was a six-year trial rather than the mentoring and cultivation of a future colleague. Either you made it, or you moved on. It mattered not a bit to our colleagues.

Mark and I shared our sorrows after hours, debated orthodox versus Western humanist Marxism, and promoted a caring attitude towards our graduate students, not least because minutes ago we, too, were in the lowest ranks of the academy. We talked incessantly about quitting the profession while still pursuing the dream of tenure.

After the Gulf War (1990–1991), Mark asked me to make a presentation in his Introduction to International Relations class. Like most of my colleagues who had asked, Mark made that mistake only once.

For my talk, I culled Third World responses to the US attack on Iraq from the pages of the *New York Times* and the *Washington Post*. I selected responses from country after country—it was a virtual circumnavigation of the globe via protest against US actions. My aim was simple but not spelled out: to show them the near unanimity of world condemnation. I did not offer my opinion nor make editorial intrusions. But my signature was certainly present in the material selected, in its editing, and in the vapid tone I took on as the nightly news anchor.

I guessed that even those against the war would, by the end of my twenty-minute presentation, be unable to bear the weight of the world against their country, a country to which even the most alienated of them would feel loyalty.

Mark's class was held in Maxwell Auditorium, a sunken half-dome that was a superb architectural space for a lecture class of 150 or so students. You walked into the room and saw in the back a curving wall of windows framed by green ivy. The entry was at the highest level, with seats terraced in below it. The stage was marked off with a three-foot drop, so as one lectured, there were students below you, at your eye-level, and above you. The seats fanned out 180 degrees to your left and right.

I sat at the center of the room, a microphone clipped to my tie, turning my pages with each report of anti-US demonstrations, or diplomatic rebukes, or quotes from various famed dissenters. I could feel their anger mounting. In the back, I caught a glimpse of Mark fighting the urge to smile.

When I stopped, without a conclusion or a coda, I knew there would be silence. I had practiced silence for years after reading Henry Kariel's brilliant piece titled simply, "Becoming Political." Five, ten, then thirty seconds went by. No one raised a hand. Just mute choppy waves of discomfort. Mark intervened, "I think what Professor Naeem is trying to say is…"

I cut him off: "Please don't feel the need to interpret me to them, Mark." The silence continued. And then, slowly, they began to defend their country—hand after hand, student after student. As one left-leaning student shared with me afterward, "You made me defend my country for the first time in my life."

* * *

The following year, our department employed a third junior professor. With our egalitarian sensibility, backed by some generous institutional financing, Mark and I formed the Maxwell International Political Economy Group (MIPEG). We were a reading group of two junior faculty and some twenty graduate students responsible for a year-long speaker series.

Our new colleague visited a few of our reading sessions but could not tolerate the mutterings of the unconfirmed. "I did not earn my Ivy League doctorate," I heard this person shout, "in order to circulate with graduate students." Twenty-seven years later, I feel the grief of this moment. Soon thereafter, MIPEG crumbled. It crushed me that something built with care, patience, and devotion could be so thoroughly destroyed.

* * *

I secretly resented the "go at it alone, sink or swim" strategy offered to fresh PhDs. So much so that when I arrived in Syracuse for my first tenure-track job, I was the only junior faculty member who complained of a lack of mentoring. The administrators pounced on my confession and produced a mentoring program.

Years later, in Ithaca, the Center for Faculty Excellence (a name so oblivious that mocking it is redundant) invited an outside expert to teach us how to excel in engaged, active, student-centered teaching. After an hour of PowerPoint slides stressing the efficacy of conversational communication, personal interactions, and specificity in learning objectives, I could no longer abide the irony: "How do you square the fact that the content of your message directly contradicts the form in which you are conveying it to us? You are the expert and yet you treat us in a manner that is orthogonal to how you would have us treat our students. Do you really expect us to take you seriously while you use PowerPoint to warn us of the dangers of lecturing?"

A few perked up, but most of my thirty-five colleagues sent me shut-down glares. Like honors students, they resented my interference in their learning experience. My intervention was breaking their note-taking rhythm.

"God save us from educators" were my last words at the workshop. The director happily accepted my suggestion that it would perhaps be best if I skipped the second day. Today, I wonder if the "sink or swim" laboratory, though inadequate, is not somehow still best. Neglect at least spares us the banality of discussions on teaching technique.

* * *

My student, Wendy Sharrit, would often visit my office. She was friendly, alert, and curious. One day, well into the semester, she asked:

"How many courses do you teach?"

"Two per semester," I responded.

"What else do you do with your time? Do you have another job?" she asked in all seriousness.

Was this conversation before or after my heart attack? I cannot recall. Probably before, when I was still under the impression that I could produce all my chair asked of me: two books at university presses, external funding, promise of future research, a successful speaker series, and a reduction in my teaching energy.

I shot up from my chair and muttered through clenched teeth, "Try shadowing me for a day. I bet you wouldn't be able to keep up."

She had no idea why I was upset. I shouldn't have been. As an undergraduate and even in graduate school, I had no idea that professors did anything besides teaching. Nor could I have imagined that teaching was largely inconsequential, the white-boiled rice on their tenure plates.

From grade school onward, students learn that their job is to read their teachers' deepest needs and satisfy their visible and hidden demands.[11] But some also have the gift of seeing and amplifying our insecurity. Rob was a kind of student legend on the third floor of Muller, and multiple professors cursed his name, simultaneously confessing that they had no choice but to give him an A for his excellent work.

He received an A for every paper he gave me in our three courses. After his third successive A in our first course, I called him into my office for two reasons. I wanted to learn how he did it, and I wanted to present him with an enhanced challenge.

The first of these was not difficult. He admitted that his huge anxiety and tremendous pressure compelled him to put in extraordinary effort. I could see all that. My second charge was more trying. I suggested that grinding out work under stress and pressure is not conducive to innovation, and I needed him to be creative. "I am sorry," he replied, "but I have to have the A."

"I'll only give you an A," I said, "if you give me a B paper." He accepted the terms, but in a way, I had failed him. He got his A by giving me a mediocre paper, but despite my attempt to relieve the pressure and give him some intellectual freedom, his effort wasn't particularly creative. I was unable to coax him out of his grind.

Many of us took his name in vain because he found our weaknesses and he named them publicly and privately. To my face, he said, "I am not some toy for your pedagogical experiments." When he left my office, but only when he left, I closed the door behind him and yelled at the chair he had just vacated, "Take your A, get out, and don't come back."

* * *

Ithaca College prizes good teaching. Formally, 60 percent of a tenure decision is based on teaching excellence. Senior faculty visit junior

---

11. ". . . there is a fissure between teacher and student that cannot be bridged. . . . The students are not learning what the teacher directly wants them to learn. They are learning from, and reacting to, what emerges in excess of the specific content." Rickert, *Acts of Enjoyment*, 2007, p. 158.

professors' classes and write an assessment that becomes part of the official file. These sessions are excruciating for the junior faculty. For the assessors, they are both fraught and tedious.

A senior colleague visited my class to assess my teaching. My student Jack saw an opportunity. Within the first ten minutes, Jack declared, with his arms flying and his voice booming, "There is no such thing as feminism." His non sequitur now delivered, he relaxed into his chair, positioning his body towards our visitor and then towards me.

His outburst produced the intended effect. My colleague braced her chair, took a deep breath, and waited to see what I would do with this random and reckless comment. She had heard about my permissive posture in the classroom, and now I could see her wondering how far I would let things go.

Jack thought he was complimenting me. His message to his former professor was: "See, in Naeem's class, I can say what I want."[12] He could not have known that it required all my reserves not to fly at his throat with two hands before I lost my job. *This couldn't have happened if I just lectured*, I thought to myself.

Jack's blundering was a precise reversal. In retrospect, I marvel at the acuity of his intuition. Often, professors deploy students into our colleagues' classrooms as guided missiles as a way to debate by proxy. Jack had inverted the play; he was deploying one professor to send a message to another.[13] My response was to suffer. I am still exhausted by the impossibility of that moment.

* * *

There are a few things I am willing to share with you about my two years of teaching at Elmira Correctional Facility. It had a permanent impact on my sensibility. All my teaching encounters have this prison

---

12. ". . . while the content of one's class may aspire to be directly liberatory, the pedagogy may perform in an authoritarian manner directly at odds with the content. Students will recognize this conflict and react to it in a variety of ways, and often that will mean forms of resistance or rejection. Perhaps even more significant, students will learn those selfsame authoritarian behaviors, even replicate them, to the extent that a teacher has legitimated them in performance." Rickert, *Acts of Enjoyment*, 2007, p. 207.

13. Kaela Bamberger has a different interpretation: "You're completely missing the competitive nature of what he did that I can so relate to—anything to annoy/anger/cause your misstep. Anything to rumble [your] infinite placidity. Anything to make you finally snap. . . . Continually pushing harder and harder only to open our eyes and hope to find you still there, calm as ever."

experience as a baseline. I was secretly overjoyed to terminate this responsibility because I was certain that one day, I would enter the facility and not walk out. I feared violence at the hands of a prisoner, a guard, or perhaps even because of a glitch in the prison's weaponized bureaucracy.

And one more thing: Bryan Nance, my teaching partner, invited me to a Barnes & Noble store to hear a young scholar giving a talk based on her prison experience. Afterward, we turned to each other in disbelief at the denatured and academic tone of the presentation. We vowed never to use our prison experience to promote our careers.

So why do I feel differently about the writing you are currently reading. Am I not doing the same with my non-prison teaching ventures?

* * *

Sally was randomly assigned to me as an advisee by the department's bureaucracy, and I failed her. Not that I didn't try. Advising is my least favorite part of the job. Not the talking and listening, because that is merely an extension of teaching. No, it's the requirements that I don't believe in that I must enforce regardless.

In her last semester, Sally announced that she was finally ready to take a course with me. I did not understand what she was trying to tell me.

One of my mottos is: "Thieves want to be caught. That is why they hide their stolen wares in plain view." Of course, they don't know that they do this. Not fully.

A week before the first paper was due, she brought in a draft for me to read, and she was not the first student to deploy this strategy. "I'm sorry," I said, "I don't do pre-reads. I need you to put in your best effort before I evaluate it officially. After that we can talk about it for as long as you like." She retreated and turned in her essay with the others.

As I finished reading her essay, I knew that we were both in trouble. Either this was an anomaly or, more likely, Sally had moved through four years of college without learning how to write. "This paper is not even at a tenth-grade level," I muttered to myself. How could this be? She was a politics major, and this meant most of her teachers were my immediate colleagues in a department that boasted the most rigorous teachers.

The next day, I walked into my colleague's office and inquired about her experience with Sally. "A fine student and wonderful person," was her summary. Betting on a whim, I asked my colleague if Sally had asked her to pre-read her papers. Sally had.

Sally's approach was ingenious. Well before the due date, she would seek help from her professors who would assist her in writing the draft. The scheme required great energy and advanced planning, and the result was good papers and good grades, but tragically, Sally failed to learn writing or reasoning.

I presented the bad news to her as two messages. My department, my colleagues, and the college had failed her. She was about to graduate without having learned how to write. Second, I would be responsible for making sure she learned how to write, even if this meant working with her after her graduation.

She never spoke to me again, but my promise still holds.

* * *

It's fall 1996, and I am teaching my first four courses at Ithaca College, including three sections of "Ideas and Ideologies." The requirements are a mid-term and final paper, or perhaps, it is three essays. I can barely recall that semester of sleep deprivation, because Sorayya and I were overtaken by waves of fevers and infections brought home by our four-year-old and transmitted to our six-month-old.

It is the last week, and somehow, we have survived the semester. A student I don't recognize walks into my office to applaud the course. Suspicious, I ask him what he likes. He enjoyed that he could turn in his papers and never need to come to class. I am alarmed. He shares that he has called all his friends and told them that mine was a class they could take without having to attend. *Oh yeah,* I think, *that's the list I want to be on.*

I redesign the course as he speaks. I explain the changes and advise him to tell his friends *not* to take my course. He is confounded: "Why would you mess with such a good thing?" he asks.

CHAPTER 4

Encounter as Method

I buy milk chocolate with almonds. My preference is bittersweet-salted dark chocolate, but this stash is not for me. I'm collecting it for the registrar. Every few years, I ferry pounds of chocolate to those who assign classroom space at our college. My needs are specific: I require double the space usually allotted to a particular enrollment number.

At first, I tried to explain why: "I arrange the chairs in a circle, and then I pace *outside* the circle. . . ." No need; they understand without explanation that my request is important to me because I meet them face-to-face. The chocolate is just a sweetener.

My associate dean didn't quite see it like that. "We can't have you bribing the registrar," she warned.

* * *

In my classes, I walk at a measured clockwise pace around the outside of the circle of chairs occupied by students. I pivot and now circle counterclockwise. With each step, the face and posture of another student come into my full view. Some students intuitively understand that the body provides ample information, so they sit poker-faced. But most of them don't notice that I am gathering, interpreting, and storing the stream of evidence they present. Nearly all my energy is devoted to ascertaining their bodily disclosures.

I find it difficult to talk/explain/present/lecture while still soaking in data from my observations of the students. This skill is not impossible for me; it emerges in those rare moments of the semester when I, too, am part of the wave, surfing it, one with its moving in totality. Mostly, though, I listen, I look, I walk, I adjust angles, alter my pace, change my direction while looking for students' commitments.

They, too, can see everyone's faces, but they are seated. There are no rows and columns, no front or back to the geometry of our circle. With each step, my angle of vision bisects the circle; I stand directly behind a student who cannot see me without turning around, and simultaneously, I am face-to-face with a student at the other end of the circle.

As each student speaks, I move to the opposite end of the circle, ensuring that the speaking student's voice is loud enough for the furthest ears and indicating that they need to address each other.

Perhaps there is an empty chair in the circle that entices me to sit. I sit, and now that my perspective is frozen, I find myself talking. Not just professor talk, but revelations—my politics, my commitments, my anger. Catching myself, I shoot up, slap my left wrist with my right hand, and declare, "Bad Professor!" As the skin-on-skin stroke reverberates in the room, the rest of my self-criticism is silent: *Stop it. You know damn well that if you show your cards, they will play only to that suit.*[1] *Then you have no chance to know them. Teach and you will not learn.*

I do not lecture, nor do I execute meticulous space-filling plans. I provide openings, I am at ease with silence, and I trust in aleatory processes—processes that go wrong in so many ways: a student is accusing another of bad faith or a lack of preparation; someone is saying something racist or sexist or otherwise offensive; someone is crying or screaming; and I am overstepping the boundary of productive risk. Some such thing goes awry every week. I worry, *My God, how will I sort out this mess.* Under such stress, half-smiling, I say in jest: "We would not have this difficulty had I just lectured the entire hour." For a long moment, I mean it.

Why can't I just do what is expected of me, what everyone else is happy to have me do, what others do? Just profess, damn it.

Professing produces predictability, secures the room for decanting knowledge, and calls forth the geometry of rows and columns, front and back, speaker and spoken to. Oh, how I long for it at that moment when I am caught frozen, standing, unsure, my heart sinking, my anger

---

1. "Teachers, in effect, say, 'If you love me, you will believe,' or 'If you want my love, you will believe.' Students who want recognition or love more than the assertion of their own desire will believe not on the basis of knowledge but on the need for recognition." Alcorn, Marshall. (2002). *Changing the Subject in English Class* (Carbondale: Southern Illinois University Press), p. 41.

at myself beginning to whistle and steam for crossing the lines of my own profession. I wait for the moment to pass.

* * *

On the first day of class, I ask the students to arrange the chairs in a circle. It is imperative for me that we all see each other's faces. The process of including all voices and all ears is built into the classroom geometry and begins immediately.

As I memorize names, I discourage pronouns; everyone must be properly named, including authors of texts. Such naming gets students in the practice of becoming precise about who they praise and criticize. I promote informality by using authors' first names and often referring to famous dead white theorists as my uncles and aunts.

On the first day, I assign the reading, but from then on, I include them in determining the pace and selection of reading assignments. Once we agree, I tell them it is a social commitment we make to each other. Crucially, I provide no grading incentives to ensure their reading, except one. If they haven't read, they will not be able to follow the discussion. Since all class time is discussion-based, they either come prepared or they absent themselves. Skipping class is easy because I have no attendance policy.

They walk into the classroom to the music I have selected for that day. After I fade out the tune, my five-minute opening includes the following script: (1) "Any problems questions, concerns, issues to be raised before we proceed?" (2) "Any announcements?" (3) "Did anyone bring needs?"

Sometimes, I will ask them if they understand why I always start this way. I need them to understand that I am ready to share the space, the control, and the power with them. At first, they treat my ritual as little more than a formal gesture. But I ask my questions every day without fail. Eventually, as the semester goes on, students do, in fact, bring needs. A biographical trauma connects to a concept, and they want to explore. They don't understand a particular passage in the reading. They wish me to explain why I have assigned a particular reading. They bring in a snippet from another class. They want to know why my course does not cover a topic that seems obviously relevant. They cannot let go of a comment someone made in the previous session.

They want to know if being in school matters at all. Their needs shape our time together.

Announcements serve to signal student investments in clubs, hobbies, and ideals. Later in the semester, some, in fact, attend or participate in each other's events. In these small ways, I am trying to produce an immanent learning community.

After the opening, I ask them (4), "How many have had the opportunity to do the reading?" I do not, and this is key, shame those that have not read because doing so deprives me of the information I seek. (Students have often told me that no other professor asks them this question.) I might also ask, (5) if they did or did not like the reading. After that, I declare: "The floor is open."

And it is.

If there is a discussion, then good. If the discussion is poor or if no one speaks, I persuade them that I will not try to save the day. I have trained myself to be silent (but inviting) in these crucial moments. Nevertheless, I might call on someone who seems eager or reveals that wheels are turning.

As we begin our work in this space, they ascertain rather quickly that they are poor conversationalists and poor readers of text. They don't know what to do about their impoverished skills. It seems that our collectivity is failing. Slowly, as they start to react to the reading and to classmates' responses, I begin to quiz them about their reactions.

My questioning never aims to take them to a particular place. I am keen for the view from their window. Almost always, I aim to strengthen their voices, to locate and articulate what they are trying to say. I interpret their muttering and ask if my translation of their words is close to what they mean.

After I have learned their names, and after I have encouraged them to articulate their responses within our deliberative public space, my job is to get the students to create a productive friction.[2] This friction is the engine of our momentum, the wind in our sails. I comment on how their various responses might be oppositional and in what ways they are harmonious. Initially, they accuse me of creating these fric-

---

2. Hannah Gignoux adds: "Or, lift the veil where their internal friction and the friction of the community always was."

tions, and they resent me for concocting alliances and enmities between them. They prefer politeness, circumspection, and vague allusions.

I explain that the highest aim of the class is not merely to learn about our putative subject matter, nor is it only to "learn how to learn." Rather, both objectives point towards a more ambitious goal, namely, learning how to create a learning community, and I tell them that becoming a good learning community requires us to argue well. I need them to fight each other with words and realize that through this friction our community develops confidence, integrity, and honesty. Without argument, we cannot thrive. I make no effort to resolve tension. If they walk out the door with it, so much the better.

There is no obligation to speak in class. There is no participation grade. My goal becomes getting the talkers to listen and the listeners to speak—if they wish. Long periods of silence are prized, and I will stop a student from breaking them if their sole motive is to overcome their discomfort with silence.

A perfect class is one in which I do not have to intervene at all, in which all or almost all the students speak, and in which we create a tension that is both unbearable and riveting. Students report headaches. Yes, that happens.

Not every student accepts what I am trying to do. In such cases, I incorporate a student's dissent as our resource. I encourage students who go against the grain of the class and challenge what they think are my positions.[3] I cloak my views and rarely intervene in matters of content.

* * *

I don't let tissue boxes run out in my office. Every week students come to cry. And sometimes colleagues. That's a tub of tears over the years. When our younger son was about eight or so, he would greet my return from the office with: "Anyone cry in your office today, dad?"

I was alarmed about this, but a visit from my friend and psychoanalyst George Hartlaub reassured me. "They cry because they can," he said. I think George meant two things. My demeanor allows it, welcomes it, possibly even provokes it. Humans laugh, they cry, they sleep, they eat. Crying takes on different forms, and it means different

---

3. "... dissensus is something to be affirmed. It is to be transvalued." Rickert, Thomas. (2007). *Acts of Enjoyment* (Pittsburgh: University of Pittsburgh Press), p. 32.

things. (As with Gato Barbieri's sax playing, if you pay attention, all hues and textures live inside the cry.)

Nevertheless, there are some days when I encounter something so powerful that I have to work on it for days and weeks before I can share it with my family. Like the day when Eddie Dowd and Paulinho Chamon took over my classroom with a profound question that changed my world.

Eddie's nine-page autobiographical essay in my "Writing and Criticism" class explored his need to justify being alive, given that he is an adopted child whose birth mother had considered an abortion. All class members had read the piece, and we'd finished a round of responses. At that moment, Paulinho intervened. Paulinho and I have traded emails trying to jog our memories. Here is how he recalls it: "I remember. . . . I was struck by the very idea of justifying my existence—even though so much of [Eddie's] piece resonated in me, that one part I simply couldn't [comprehend]. I never considered, in my worst moment of self-deprecation, that I needed to justify existing in the world."

Paulinho called for a "lightning round," which is when I ask everyone to respond to a thought. Paulinho asked everyone whether they felt they had to justify their existence or not.

I anticipated that perhaps three of the twenty-five people in the room would respond with, "Yes, I really don't think I deserve to be alive, and therefore, I need to find reasons to justify my continued existence." The results were unexpected; the poll revealed we were evenly split.

Three elements stupefied me on that day. First, the numbers themselves. Second, I could not predict their responses even though I thought I knew most of them well from multiple semesters of working together. Finally, and most importantly, there was hardly any communication across this divide. Those of us on the "I have never considered having to validate my existence" side couldn't fathom the wearisome misery of continuous justification. And those who daily contemplate their potential nonexistence did not understand what life might be like for those for whom it is not a question.

Logically, there should be a middle ground here, right? But there wasn't. Either you never thought of it, or the thought never left you. Two planets separated by a vacuum.

That event exposed my limits. I had never contemplated that any-one's life needed justification. I realized that I didn't really know half my students.

* * *

Paul Levigne was tall, athletic, and intense. He played tennis for the college, and he was serious about his college experience. I could tell from his frown that he was about to yell at me.

I was in my room, 325 Muller, for office hours. I don't give appoint-ment times; it is first come, first served. My policy is to provide as much time as each student needs, whether five or twenty-five minutes. I require that my door be left open when students visit unless they insist on closing it.

My room is cramped. The east wall is lined with books from floor to ceiling. Invariably, students are impressed and often intimidated by the sheer number of volumes. They ask: "Have you read all of these?" Or, "How many of these have you read?" My answer depends on my mood, which ranges from playful to brief. I might simply reply that no, I have not read them all. I might say that the better question is, "How many have I re-read." I might ask the student to point randomly at three or five books and ask me if I have read those. Or, I might ask, "What are you really asking?"

The west wall is lined by two desks: a long one with various drawers and a short one that serves as a computer stand. The space between these two walls is no more than ten feet. The north wall is centered by a two-foot-wide window that runs from floor to ceiling and offers a spectacu-lar view of Cayuga Lake. My chair is set slightly away from the window so as to not obstruct the students' view when they sit in the middle of my office. Sometimes I can fit two chairs there but never three. The students get the lake view, and I can look through the open door on the south side allowing me to see how many students are waiting in the lounge. To my east and west are professors' offices; more offices line the other side of the hallway and waiting room. Indeed, the entire floor is little more than a long series of concrete cubicles usually occupied by members of the English department and the Politics department.

The walls are by no means thin, but I have been asked to turn down the volume of my music and conversations. The "Third Worlder" in me is not particularly concerned with such sensitivities. Nearby colleagues have had to acculturate themselves to the music and the shouting. Besides books and music, my office is full of the yelling and tears that result from my pedagogical decisions.

For three weeks, Paul has been waiting for my teaching to start. He recognizes nothing I have done as "instruction." He has had to listen to students speak on our readings and follow their seemingly aimless debates. I am sympathetic to his problem.

I once took a summer course at Michigan State University in which a retired professor's idea of preparation was to offer commentary on the headlines of the *New York Times*. Finally, an older student stood up and berated the professor. As the student walked out, the professor turned to the rest of us and asked if we felt likewise. I did, but I lacked the courage to step forth.

So, I admire Paul's gusto. This is a delicate moment for me. I try to explain my method, but you cannot see what you cannot see; we observe only what we know to observe. Much, if not all, of our perception depends on expectations. Knowing is seeing.

In the third week of July, I make a pilgrimage to the Finger Lakes GrassRoots Festival of Music. It is famed for its intergenerational crowd, from babies to white-haired hippies, but it is also marked by whiteness, especially in the selection of bands. Still, the organizers make a token effort to incorporate international acts. For example, Djelimady Tounkara and the Super Rail Band, from Mali. The announcer introduces Tounkara as Africa's finest guitarist. I am almost beside myself in anticipation, expecting some other-worldly version of Jimi Hendrix, Carlos Santana, and John McLaughlin. I am baffled when the entire set goes by without what I could discern as a solo. It was only when, ten years later, I learned the difference between a transcendent and an immanent solo, that I realized what I had missed. In jazz, a tradition in which I was steeped, transcendent solos are admired and perfected. They showcase technical and expressive virtuosity that lifts the audience into states of ecstasy. In the West African tradition, by contrast, the point of the virtuoso is to be with others: to play so as to accent and highlight the offerings of the rest of the band members, to signal others' contributions, and to incorporate the audience as part of the performance. The soloist, rather than kinetically doing something *to* the listener, brings everyone into the occasion *as* a participant.

I explain to Paul that I wasn't doing nothing. He just did not yet recognize what I was doing, namely, the immanent playing that points to others. He left angry, of course.

Two weeks later, he was back, and this time he let me have it in full blast for everyone to hear. I was not taking my teaching responsibility seriously. I was wasting his time. I was squandering his money. He needed me to start teaching. His critique was fully audible three offices away, but that was not what concerned me. In his actions, I recognized an element of bullying. An action, I am ashamed to report, that I had in my college days perpetrated against an aging history professor.

Bullying actions are calls that are meant to invite a response. In fourth grade, Charlie hunted me after school every day for months. My friends and I concocted elaborate plans for my 3:15 PM escapes. One day, I was cornered, and before I knew it, my fists had landed punches on his chin, as if by their own volition. He froze in disbelief, and I escaped past his astonishment. His surprise surprised me. Subsequently, from fifth to seventh grade, he expressed only one wish: to be my friend. I don't tell this story to promote violence; rather, I am trying to ascertain the bully's secret wish, namely, to find someone who will draw a line.

I knew I had to match Paul's volume and emotion: "Drop the fucking course then. Either get with my program or find someone else who fits your needs." All said in a volume heard four offices away. He did not drop the course.

* * *

I am teaching "Ideas and Ideologies" in the southeast corner of Williams Hall where the south-facing windows also open to the loading dock for the cafeteria. Trucks idle there. Their low hum interferes with my effort to hear the nuance of student conversations. I take the five minutes to walk down and ask the driver to turn off the engine. Returning to class, I see that they have conspired in my absence. It is late in the semester, and they want to hear me speak. We have worked through a series of "-isms"—liberalism, conservatism, fascism, anarchism, feminism, and socialism. They wish to know where I stand, and they want to know how to synthesize these materials. I've hinted that I will lecture if they ask me.

I prepare my materials with a nostalgia for the yellow notepads I once filled up at the beginning of my career. Hundreds of pages of lecture notes were proof of my productivity. In class, I am eager, articulate, and enjoying my presentation. I know that I am "on." They seem pleased to finally hear me, unadulterated. But the *rhythm* is the thing, you see. Ten minutes in, a student interrupts me. Then another. And now there are five of them conversing with each other—back to their own tempo. What about the lecture I prepared?

* * *

Universal Rules of conversation:[4]

Interruptions are common and necessary;
If two are conversing, there are two who don't know what they are saying;
If two are conversing, there are two not listening.
These propositions make conversation possible.

* * *

Margaret Himley, then a writing professor, was a member of both of my team-teaching experiences. She visited my small section of twenty students and watched us work. After class, she seemed amused. "You don't cover, do you?"

I didn't understand.

"I mean," she clarified, "you didn't have the students go over the reading assignment."

I defended: "I assigned the reading, which they likely read, but our conversation didn't go that way. What we ended up talking about instead seemed more important."

"That's what I mean," she said. "You didn't feel compelled to cover the reading."

Hmmmmm, I thought. Words make things. Margaret gave me vocabulary for an element of my method. And she made me feel less alien to myself.

* * *

---

4. Developed with Laura Oriol.

Among my teaching pleasures are moments when conversation cannot be contained within the circle. A side conversation breaks out, and I try not to be annoyed that I am listening to two of them. Perhaps a third and fourth source emerge, and sometimes, the entire room is ablaze in multiple vocalizations.

My favorite of these moments was in Rio when suddenly the entire room not only erupted in numerous conversations, but they also returned to Portuguese. I heard it not as chatter but as music. When you don't understand the meaning of words, it is easier to hear them as reverberations. I stood back, closed my inner eye, and let their music move through me. After a few glorious moments, one of them broke the trance: "For the sake of the professor, we should speak in English." They ignore him. Finally, they reemerge into the formality of our space. They are surprised at my amusement: Haven't they just excluded me?

But there are greater pleasures still, those of collective improvisation, where they and I work as a team to take us through ideas that have seemed just beyond our reach all semester.

In my second version of "Race and International Relations" at Ithaca College, we came across many such moments, nevertheless on the day of our final meeting, we pushed well beyond. We had already established the disabling costs of learning. That day, somehow, we were pushing beyond to the next questions: "If learning is so painful, why do we persist? What do we gain when we learn?"

First, we listed a few costs of learning. The world is structured by tragedy, and we human beings fail at almost everything we do. It is not because we lack resolve or intelligence but merely because the law of unintended consequences makes planned change a near impossibility. Second, the more we learned, the fewer people we could name as friends. Knowing leads to aloneness and even to loneliness.

I recall one summer long ago when family was visiting, and I was desperate to produce a draft of a book. I spent three months in my office reading and writing while listening on auto-repeat to Chucho Valdés' albums *Religion of the Congo* and *Bele Bele en La Habana*. One evening, Sorayya said, "You don't see anyone all day." It was a complaint, a declaration, and a question. I thought about it back in the office and confirmed her observation. But I also realized that I instead communed with the words of dead writers. Good company, and a fair trade.

Another cost of knowing is the most defeating. Namely, knowing eviscerates our innocence and denies simple linear trajectories towards heroism. Once we acknowledge that we cannot but be complicit in the very structures we wish to change (capitalism, racism, sexism, etc.), we lose something forever, namely our innocence and our drive for the immediate solutions.

The students in "Race and International Relations" were a stoic group. They didn't need the slow, pulverizing energy that I usually had to bring in order for students to consider such claims. Which is perhaps why we were able to make the next move.

I/we/they came up with a list of four advantages. First, if we push through the pain of knowing, we gain clarity. We see the world with fewer illusions and attain a kind of sparkling accuracy in our lives. Second, we can connect better. When, by studying various global structures, we grasp our holistic connectivity with others, we reduce our judgment over others, and they become easier for us to access as parts of ourselves. Susan Griffin, in her poem "Happiness" (1986), which I saw posted on a wall while teaching in Elmira Correctional Facility, writes: "This/ is the paradox of vision:/ Sharp perception softens/ our existence in the world."

Third, we chisel meaning into the block randomness of the world. Finally, there is relief that comes in accepting that we have always known that the world is a world of tragedy. Without this relief, we waste energy asserting hopefulness.

* * *

I sent this list of the costs and benefits of learning to my former student, Laura Oriol. Long ago, Laura understood that a pedagogy of encounter is not limited by the formality of registration, the temporal limits of a semester, or spatial ones of a classroom. She often sent me her writing from Toronto, then from Portland, and lately from Paris. Recently, she moved back to Ithaca for a month, and we met twice a week to talk about teaching, learning, and the body as a source of knowledge.

She added to what we *gain* when we suffer through learning: energy, joy and humor, and a reflexive understanding of our contradictions.

We retain energy, she writes, by not wasting energy covering up painful things. We receive gifts of joy and humor, she says, because learning creates a fertile ground for them. It offers a reflective and critical but also forgiving space. When we feel safe, we can take risks, we loosen our bodies, and we do not hold on to our beliefs so tightly.

Joy emerges, she explains, when we sit with our pain. This joy is related to compassion. The labor of uncovering our illusions can be joyful because, as we labor, we better internalize the connectedness that is revealed to us. Humor particularizes the moment; it can help us relate to our experience of the world with humility. Through humor, we can approach conflict and friction with joy because we suspect that friction and conflict are encounters that will lead us to our desires. All this gives us access to an unpretentious reflexivity.

Laura points out that our time together is punctuated by abundant laughter. She recalls our classes similarly. *It's true*, I think, *we laugh a lot*. But Laura has to point this out to me, perhaps because I fret too much over the damage I am causing as I systematically burst their bubbles about our ability to change the world. I overlook the sheer fun and delight in working through ideas in each other's company.

* * *

Between the eighth and twelfth week[5] of a college semester, something magical happens. Students begin to bond as a learning community. There is a visible respect and genuine curiosity with which they speak to each other. They begin to write well, read carefully, and to enjoy our time together.

I call it "magic" because I am still not sure how it happens and because sometimes, it doesn't happen. The magic requires a set of conditions that are immanent to each emerging community—the time, the place, the course materials, the people, and our interactions. All elements must congeal. When things go well, I know that four things have happened. We have addressed some putative subject matter. We have confronted the difficulties and impossibility of learning. We have considered the need to make the learning process more central to our lives, and we have absorbed what it takes to enter and to form a learn-

---

5. Out of fifteen weeks, usually.

ing community. What remains a mystery to me is how these properties emerge within a particular classroom.

* * *

Not everything happens in the classroom. Much also takes place within the cycles of the writing relationship and during office hours. In addition to not giving paper topics, I usually do not assign grades on their first papers.

I provide an abundance of comments on their papers. However, initially, rather than give them a poor grade, I will refrain from posting a mark and instead ask them to come to office hours. Often this means that more than half the class will need to see me after their first paper. I recall one honors class in which eighteen of twenty students received "no grade." I then spend fifteen minutes or more going over their paper with them. If they wish, they can rewrite their paper. Thus, rewriting is built into the course design, a labor-intensive process.

* * *

Connor Mullane was masquerading as a "B-" student. He thought only about war's violence. He played war games at all hours, traveled distances to reenact famous battles, and incessantly read war novels. War captivated and repulsed him. Connor's problem was that his curiosity and motivation emerged *only* in the presence of this topic. He couldn't be moved by grades or the pull of a future career.

When, finally, I understood this, our course subject matter became irrelevant. He devoured whole books within days (Sven Lindqvist's *The History of Bombing*, Michael Scheuer's *Imperial Hubris*, Svetlana Alexievich's *Zinky Boys*). He wrote supplemental papers and made it a habit to come by my office to sort out his thinking.

We gave his obsession a more respectable name: curiosity. He had always been working on his own project, but school thwarted his energy rather than releasing it. School bored him. There was no point, however, in blaming the institution since it merely performed its function.

* * *

Late in the semester, perhaps after the first indications that my students are making themselves into some kind of learning community, I confront them with their own desire. Perhaps it's a crisp sunny day, and I think, *Why aren't they outdoors playing?*

I have probably already dashed their easy hopes for making the world a better place. The readings and discussions seem merciless on that prospect. I ask them to consider how our intent and our plans are offset by those of others working in the opposite direction. I have placed before them theories of spontaneous order and disorder that show them how order and disorder can emerge from the actions and interactions of thousands and millions of people without anyone's intent. I demonstrate our necessary complicity in the very oppressions we work to overcome. I present macro- and micro-structures that sustain their shapes over decades and centuries despite our desire to have them be otherwise. The complexities of the world are so daunting and our abilities so feeble, I suggest, that we are unlikely to see in our lives any of the changes we seek. We cannot be sure, I conjecture, that we frame the problems correctly. It is not just their commitment to fair weather activism that I uncover. "What use is learning if that knowledge is as insignificant as it seems?" I ask. I offer myself as a prime example. "I have studied global structural inequality for more than three decades," I say, "and my understanding of what to do about it is far less sure than when I began."

As I expose the hollowness of their bright shiny enthusiasm, they drop from the sky like birds who are no longer willing to flap their wings. Those who feel beaten stop attending. Those attending seem to have no reason to come. We arrive at a moment of loss. It feels like too much.

Finally, I ask: "Since making the world a better place seems so hopeless, why not just party?"

Inevitably, they laugh at my gambit, not yet having grasped the ominousness of the trap I have set. Dozens of times, I have poked them with the thought that good students don't avoid the professor's trap; good students use their own bodies to spring the trap. Why? In order to see what happens. After all, it's only a classroom—a hypothetical, utopic, ideal setting compared to the world outside.

"You could enjoy the day, so why did you come?"

"There is no attendance policy, so why are you here?"

"If the world is hopeless, then why don't we all just enjoy our-selves?"

They laugh, and inevitably someone says, "But we are already party-ing. That's what dorms are for."

I don't laugh. My practiced tone is just short of somber, my pac-ing is deliberate, and I am riffing a ballad in the lower registers of the baritone sax.

I don't want to press this moment. I let them linger on the hints about how their partying bores them while our partying brings them in even on this rare cloudless Ithaca day.

My riff is a tease, not a consummation. I will bring it up again.

* * *

One of my favorite moments is to ask the following question at the right time: "If you knew for sure that your effort to change the world would not lead to any results within your lifetime, would you sustain the effort?"

They cannot see that I am setting upon a long-term trek. I record their answers in my memory, and then at the end of the semester, I revisit the question by saying, "If your answer to this question is 'no,' then you are a hope junky, and I want nothing to do with you. But if your answer is 'yes,' then we can work together, perhaps next semes-ter."[6] I know I am testing their faith in faith.

* * *

Kadyr Toktogulov was a visiting student from Kyrgyzstan in my "International Conflict" course. He recounted how his parents fondly recollected the days when Kyrgyzstan was part of the USSR. My stu-dents found this nostalgia impossible to grasp, so they questioned him. Kadyr, who I would see again many years later, miraculously meeting inside Istanbul's Blue Mosque, kept looking at me wondering if he was taking up too much class time in his defense of what Sovietization and

---

6. Laurence Dickey on grace: "It was not within man's power to command, participate in, or expect grace: that was God's prerogative; and the ultimate test of faith was to preserve in one's faith without any guarantee of salvation. The mystery of grace was, as God was, inscrutable. For that reason Augustine put faith at the very 'heart' of his theology and tied it to man's affec-tive faculty." Dickey, Laurence. (1987). *Hegel: Religion, Economics, and the Politics of Spirit, 1770–1807* (Cambridge: Cambridge University Press), p. 31.

modernization had brought to his part of central Asia. I gave him the time he needed, and he schooled us.

* * *

Jason Gabari comes to class in a full Superman outfit: boots, blue tights, the big S on his chest, and the flowing red cape. He also carries a small frying pan. Every day, in Job Hall, he raises his frying pan to ask questions and make comments in a tone of understated sincerity. I play along happily, mirroring his indifference to his self-presentation. Until, late in the semester, I finally ask, "Jay, I get the Superman outfit [I didn't], but why the frying pan?" He responds, "Each time someone says something stupid, I hit myself with it." He had, I thought, an intuitive grasp of healing. I take his pan with me everywhere I go.

* * *

Brandy Heath offered five written pieces for the class to read when I taught "Writing and Criticism" for the first time. Initially, like the other students, she was reluctant, but once she understood what the course asked of her, the words flowed. She used the course to work out how to respond to her life situation. Brandy reported that when she was a child, her black mother opted for drug use and refused treatment for mental illness, which required Brandy's family to sever ties with her.

Meanwhile, her white father raised Brandy and her brother but revealed his patriarchal and racist views. No one was allowed to question his performance as a father, despite his racism, sexism, homophobia, demeaning control, manipulation, and verbal abuse. In fact, he considered himself a savior to his two children despite insinuating that he, too, might abandon them.

Brandy's professors were clear about her options when she shared with them this structural impossibility. They told her she needed to disavow her father. She understood their logic, but she subconsciously rejected this resolution as a betrayal. When she sketched this story to me, I suggested that she build on this rift, engage the contradiction, and release herself from the need to produce a solution. She had, of course, known this all along and had been waiting for someone to nudge her towards this alternative. Suddenly, she wrote prolifically, and it is only a slight exaggeration to say that we co-convened that course.[7]

* * *

In *Resistance to Learning*, Marshall Alcorn writes, "The work of thought is not like driving a nail into a piece of lumber." Rather, teaching involves a "complex resituating of thought in new contexts where different emotional attitudes allow reflective cognitive consolidation. You cannot drive thought into a mind of a thinker."[8] However, what we can do is change contexts. For example, we can discuss British imperialism in the nineteenth century when the target is US imperialism in the twenty-first. This change allows "an anxious thought to become drained of its attendant anxiety."[9]

Translation: teaching works analogically. Making a point requires us to travel away from it. Teaching is, therefore, a branch of a theory of travel. Hammering a nail into its target, on the other hand, speaks to the teacher's anxiety, to the teacher's inability to trust in travel.

* * *

Renee sat quietly for most of the semester in my "Origins of Global Fury" course. Besides being the only hard sciences major, she was also the only foreigner. The less she said, the more powerful the students

---

7. Brandy Heath replies: "I also was grateful for reading Kiese Laymon's *How to Slowly Kill Yourself and Others in America: A Remembrance*. I found in this piece a medium to best express the cycles of my story. There's this censoring that regularly happens inside myself to paint the perfectly told version of my life. I found myself submitting pieces of my hardships that I myself didn't believe. Laymon's piece gave me the opportunity to unapologetically insert myself into my own stories.

I remember being so angry that your course [Writing and Criticism] demanded me to be authentic to myself. Like I hadn't spent the past four years doing the most intensive work of self-reflection. I can't remember the first piece I "offered," but I remember picking it because someone else told me it was good enough to deserve a grade of 98. It was a recycled story repeatedly granting me praise without ever having to dig into who I was on the paper. When I was finally told the story was as recycled and meaningless as it had become to me during your course, I was terrified. I submitted the offering because if it was to be criticized by strangers, I'd be comfortable with them tearing apart something that wasn't really me. However, as the critiques continued and evolved, I was terrified by the realization that everyone around the room was demanding my authentic story. Somehow, my dad's fatherhood was put into question, a questioning I had grown up resisting and subduing. A questioning if I openly spoke about would result in me losing a savior I so desperately needed to live."

8. Alcorn, Marshall. (2013). *Resistance to Learning* (New York: Palgrave Macmillan), p. 58.

9. Alcorn, *Resistance to Learning*, p. 59.

made her persona. She eventually had to speak because they kept turning to her.

My first problem was how to get the students to understand that the rest of the world did not think of the United States in benign terms. Yes, they wished access to its wealth, its educational institutions, and its promise of meritocratic mobility, but this did not mean that they thought of their own culture as lesser or US culture as superior.

No matter their liberal bent, I always assume in my students an inborn sense of cultural superiority, but I cannot use my "Third World" experience as a trump card. That would amount to silencing them. My second problem was how to create space where we might consider that masters have shortcomings and servants have proficiencies. Renee took care of both my problems when she finally spoke.

She pronounced with a vehemence and intensity, "Thank God, I was not born in this country." The other students sprang back, and after a few deep breaths, they needed to know what exactly she meant. "Why?" they asked, preparing themselves. "Because," she said, "then I would be like you all, unable to realize how much the rest of the world hates you." Her words floored her classmates, but I doubt if what she said came as a revelation. After all, they had created the conditions of this moment of anticipated surprise.

It means much less if the same message comes from the readings or from the professor. Hearing it from a peer is decisive in shifting towards unacknowledged and unoccupied theoretical space.

* * *

About ten weeks into my "Theories of Exploitation" course, Jasmine Gayle suggests something like this:

"I know that there is nothing in patriarchy that I could ever like. It negates me. I know, even more viscerally, that there is nothing in the system of racism that I can appreciate. It, too, negates me. But in a different way than patriarchy. Capitalism, however, holds out some allure even though I know I don't like it and even though I know that it is wrong. It is in me like a promise of something good."

For years, I've been working on the difference between the *naturalized* hierarchy that supports sexism and white supremacy versus the *social* hierarchy that meritocracy and capitalism enable. And all at once, Jasmine gives me what I am looking for.

* * *

I announce in the middle of class with a large smile, "I cultivate and gain your trust. Then I betray it. That is my *modus operandi*. You've been warned." With this, I gain their trust, which, of course, I will betray should the pedagogical moment call for it. I hope to do this, somehow, without losing their faith.

* * *

Nicole's work forced me to recognize how much I was asking of my students. In my "Afghanistan and the Origins of Global Fury" course, we studied how much destruction the British and US empires had caused the Third World. Nicole's paper revealed that her great grandfather and two grandfathers fought in World War I, World War II, and in Korea. She was named after her paternal grandfather, whose footlocker was bequeathed to her. It contained photo albums, medals, dress uniforms, a first aid kit, flags, and a war-time journal, as well as war trophies taken from German soldiers. Her loved ones bequeathed to her a sacred pride in family military history. It was not easy for her to read, much less write about, the predicament in which my course placed her.

As she disclosed details in her writing, she allowed me to feel her anguish as she considered that besides the honor and nobility of her family's sacrifice lay their culpability in possible war crimes. The work that she was willing to do was tearing apart her world.[10]

I cautioned myself. Pushing her more would cause me to lose her. Pushing her more was ethically unjustifiable. Pushing her more was wasteful. All that.

* * *

Justin was among the students willing to out himself in my office as "working class." Ithaca College students, overall, have plenty of discretionary income that they flaunt, knowingly and unknowingly. Is-

---

10. Laura McNeal responds: "Is there a place for what and whom she loved and for the damage to co-exist? Wallace Stevens and the principle of innocence always comes to mind for me: 'There may be always a time of innocence. There is never a place.'"

sues of race and gender are common currency in our classrooms, both as subject matter and as identity markers. "Class," on the other hand, is hidden.

While in my "Cuba and Haiti" course, Justin became fascinated with economic rights and enthusiastically contrasted the life of working-class US citizens with Cuban life. He was insightful and thorough in his criticisms of the United States and in his appreciation for Cuban principles. Yet, he hesitated when I pressed the class with a thought experiment. Assume that you are about to be born and that you can select the location. Do you select the United States or Cuba?

Unlike other students, Justin immediately understood the probabilities. In the United States, you had a chance of total destitution and a chance for billionaire-hood. In Cuba, neither option was possible, and your range of income mobility, at its best, was only six times greater than what the lowest person earned. Justin grasped that the rational decision was to select Cuba, but he selected the United States.

He agreed to write his final paper on this tension. The results were agonizing for both of us. He confessed that he could not let go of the chance to make it big even if the odds were against him and the consequences were dire. Of course, his response is socialized by his upbringing in the United States. But I think it is also suggestive of something more. I am trying to identify what that might be.

* * *

It is the fall semester in 1996. I am forty and a decade into my teaching career but starting anew on a one-year contract at Ithaca College after failure at Syracuse University. Nora was my student from my very first semester at Ithaca. She was bold, loud, confident, and smart. The former high school cheerleader negotiated male desire with assurance that was second nature to her. She once accused me of creating an asexual space in my office hours. She took six courses with me in which she wrote seamlessly about politics and her personal life. Her essays carefully and theoretically unfolded her childhood sexual abuse.

We developed close ties, and she was often in our home as a babysitter to our two young children. Later, a career in humanitarian aid allowed her to travel the world. She is the only one of my former students who has visited my parents' home in Islamabad.

Nora didn't mind shouting at me, and I enjoyed yelling back—with the office door open, of course. My department chair walked by during one such interaction, detected our intimacy, and jumped to a conclusion. My teaching methods were already creating waves within the department. My chair, instrumental in my hiring, came to regret her enthusiasm for me. One day, while I was about to get into my car in the parking lot in front of Muller, she walked over to me and declared, "You have too strong an influence on your students, especially the women."

I froze, as is my penchant in such moments. I heard the threat and the command. She was suggesting I change my ways, or it might be my only year at Ithaca College. That shook me. Having just left Syracuse University, could I afford to buck my new chair?

I conveyed to Nora that I would have to renege on my promise to include her essay in my reader for the following semester. She was stupefied and berated me for my lack of courage. "If my work is good enough, why can't you publish it?" she rightly demanded.

Many days later, after considerable deliberation with Sorayya, I went to my chair's office and informed her, "I can become better at my methods, but I cannot change them."

* * *

Sometimes they catch me not doing my job. Five times in my career, students have come to my office to say, as Betsy Aleshire did, "You are not taking me seriously enough. I need better and more detailed critique. You are underestimating me." Each time, in silence, I pled guilty to their accusation, took back the marked paper, and promised a more thorough reading. I don't know how they can see in me what I cannot see in myself. I don't know how they can muster the resolve to demand more of me or how they humble themselves so earnestly. It's a kind of greatness, I'd say.

* * *

I tell my honors classes that I don't like honors students. It is also a chance to share a tool, the ecological fallacy: "Just because I don't like the category nor the plurality of honors students does not mean that I won't like you," I say. I wonder why I am compelled to alienate them on the first day. Perhaps I am trying to warn them that their sheen and shine alone will not do.

Professors, themselves invariably former honors students, especially dislike my public denouncements of such students. I was one—but in my defense, I didn't like myself for it.

Only twice has my public declaration been explicitly appreciated. Brooke Reynolds stepped up and asked about my problem with honors students. I laughed and said that I did not find them distractable. "Not distractable? What does that mean?" she asked. "I mean," I said, "that I find them difficult to distract into learning." And, Katie Stimson, shared: "You reached inside me and turned something off." Turned off the desire to compete and shine, I hoped.

* * *

Giving students minimal prompts—"Write about something you think is important to you"—requires repetition. I give them my reasoning: when we professors provide you with questions for your essay topics, we deprive you of the opportunity to formulate your own questions. In class, the logic sounds reasonable, but then students come to my office and say, "But I don't know what to ask."

I elaborate: "I assume everyone *comes* to college already with a full project buried within their body. Our job, my job, is not to teach you anything. My job is to get you to bring that project out of you and into the open."[11] This doesn't help, of course. Students leave my office just as baffled as before.

The skills students need to produce, say, a substantial research paper includes the usual organizing, rewriting, building bibliographies, anticipating counterarguments, and so on, but none of that comes without prior motivation. And the prior motivation is either the fear of failure or hope of success. The skill I hope to unfold in the student is how to excavate the questions that are already inside them.

---

11. "Sure, there is no correlative, harmonious teacher-student relation, but perhaps this pedagogical fissure can be seen to work for us, to enable us in productive ways. . . . Pedagogy could reflect this concern [that our pedagogy has unintended and unknown consequences] by promoting the idea that each student life is its own *telos*: the individual struggles of each student cannot and should not necessarily mirror our own." Rickert, *Acts of Enjoyment* p. 2007, 164–65.

Uncovering this skill, however, is not simply a matter of hearing me talk and then making changes. Why? Because making these changes requires nothing less than a comprehensive remaking of college education.

CHAPTER 5

Consequences

Encounter and Risk

Julia Guimaraes expected to excel in my six-week class in Rio. She wrote four short papers, and I graded none of them. Or, in her words, she received "un-grades." Two weeks left in the course with no grades produced panic in her. In my office, she expressed grave concern for her funding and for her future should she receive a poor grade from me, although she wasn't the only one in our course I had placed in this situation.

"Julia," I said, "I know that you hate the course. So why don't we start there." She insisted I was wrong; she hated neither the course nor my methods and certainly not the professor. Fifteen minutes later, we agreed that she detested doing the short papers and that my pedagogy confused her. I countered, "If you can agree that behind your confusion there is irritation and perhaps a vehement dislike, then perhaps we can get somewhere."[1]

Recall my claim that one builds *on* the rift, *on* the fissure.

Then, in two long papers, she delivered a formidable critique of my teaching. My method, she explained, was to get the student to understand that all their previous work was a process that alienated their own curiosity and desire. I undermined and destroyed all that and asked instead for thinking and writing that revealed how the student had de-alienated themselves. But how was this fair when everyone else in the educational institution groomed students to alienate themselves? Was

---

1. ". . . inventive resistance to control is always happening. Perhaps key here is less the necessity of trying to produce its possibility . . . than trying simply to recognize it." Rickert, Thomas. (2007). *Acts of Enjoyment* (Pittsburgh: University of Pittsburgh Press), p. 197.

not my teaching, or to use her words, my "unteaching," counter-productive towards the aims and goals of acquiring a job and a profession?

Was not my method, she continued, just another preconceived formula, another form of imperialism? Further, my methods misunderstood the positive power of authority, which the teacher could use to challenge students. She wanted to sustain the status quo that she had deciphered and that her skills had perfected as a top student in an elite institution. Who was I to undermine years and years of careful planning?

My vague prompts and my open cultivation of paradox and uncertainty, she argued, allowed students to evade deeper questions. I misunderstood my own method; instead of producing de-alienation, I was facilitating it. As I commented on her paper, "Ouch!"

I am still dealing with implications of her critique. In part, I recognized this line of reasoning because I've heard hints of it from others: working-class students who demand an actual learning product from our interaction (for example, the attainment of some specific knowledge and skill). And, honors students, or honors-ish students—those who excel by means of perfecting the art of self-alienation to meet professors' needs—are flummoxed and disarranged when they cannot solve my unholy challenge. Like Julia, they demand a return to the status quo.[2]

As my friend and colleague Don Beachler enjoys pointing out, my classes don't work for everyone.

Julia's critique awed me because she showed me the limits of a process that I was trying to make explicit and that remains elusive to me.

* * *

In the hallway after my first day of class at the International Relations Institute in PUC-Rio, Ana Carolina Delgado, the most senior of the graduate students enrolled in my class, and herself teaching courses, looked me squarely in the eye and asked, "Do you know what you are doing?" I noted the blend of reproach and concern in her question.

---

2. "There is a loss in this [thinking of product as process] that may be hard to bear for those now in authority. After all, they are asked to welcome a transfer of trust to whatever groping figures might join courses. . . . To what extent can we support instructors who fail (as we still say) to structure courses prior to the first day of class?"Kariel, Henry. (1977). "Becoming Political," in Vernon van Dyke (ed.), Teaching Political Science (London: Humanities Press), p. 142–4.

My classroom in Rio de Janeiro was the size of my dining room and living room combined—perhaps no more than 500 square feet. Twenty-five students sat around the walls of the room, the closest we came to forming the circle I needed. There was nowhere for me to move; all I had left was to shift my weight from leg to leg.

I was the foreign expert hired to teach a six-week course on "International Inequality." The professor who promised to bring me to Rio, Nizar Missari, had moved to a university in Morocco. His writing partner, who, like me, is an alum of the University of Denver, was my direct host. Nizar had told me at ISA, "You know, in Rio, we read your book." I didn't believe him. But here was the proof; many of the masters and doctoral students had read *International Relations and the Problem of Difference* and were just as eager to read the new book, *Savage Economics*.[3]

It was a profound pleasure for me to escape the Anglophile teaching landscape and arrive in this pocket of familiarity. I'd lived in Kuala Lumpur, so I happily breathed in the warmth, the humidity, and the tropical verdure. I'd lived in Pakistan, so I felt at home in the anarchy of the traffic. I'd collected Brazilian music, so I savored the poetry of spoken Portuguese. I'd always represented the Third World, so I imagined that my students would be at ease with me.

In class, I made my first mistake immediately, and it defined our interaction. As I stood in front of the students, they seemed tense but also eager to be good hosts. I wanted to reduce their anxiety a notch, so I said, "Please, there is no need for you to provide me with that Third World sense of hospitality." I meant it in only the most affirming terms.

I had misunderstood my audience. Most of them took it as a slight and were either hurt or offended. Did I know, they asked, that Brazil exported not just airplanes but also knowledge, that Brazil had one of the world's largest economies and was becoming a major player in international decisions?

I had always considered Brazil as a leader and champion of the "Third World," whereas they assumed that Brazil was now at the cusp of "First World" status.

---

3. Both books are co-authored with David L. Blaney.

An aside: In the late 1970s, I was staying in my parents' home in Kuala Lumpur, watching the evening news with my family. The anchor announced that Malaysia had reached the per capita income required to attain "First World" status. With that, suddenly, Malaysia attained the rank so coveted by all former colonies. I laughed out loud at the sonic arrival, but I also marveled at the conviction. This moment is both vacuous and tangible.

My mistake with my new students immediately revealed the actual rift between us. Some students agreed that Brazil was "Third World-ish," and of these, some even relished this station. Later, many were aghast when some of the readings favorably mentioned Cuban ideals of economic justice. Brazil, they thought, had little to learn from such a puny member of the international community.

As has been my intuitive habit, later developed into a principle, I built our discussions *on* the rift between us. The principle might be succinctly expressed as, *The difference is the debate.* I teased them about their aspirations to be recognized as developed, modern, and grand. Meanwhile, they wondered how a Pakistani housed in the West had anything to say about Brazil's location in the world hierarchy. Our familial scrimmage simmered alongside their ingrained respect for my authority as an imported professor and their continued need to see themselves as gracious hosts.

To fully describe my experience with these students and to do justice to the intensity and love in this exchange would require a space of its own, so great was their impact on me. When on the last day of class, they seemed to ask, in many little ways, how their performance rated in my experience, I was (rightly, I think) hesitant to provide an answer. Not because I enjoy any part of being the "withholding father," a ubiquitous and tired role played by so many of my senior colleagues. But because I did not yet know that I had fallen in love. I needed time to fathom the textures of our experience and to savor the flavors of our interactions.

Ten years later, I know that visits by some of these students to our home in the backwater tundra that is Ithaca have been extravaganzas for my family and me and that my continued interaction with this cohort is even richer than the original singular experience.

I shower this group with acclaim, not because other cohorts—in Colorado, in Syracuse, in Elmira, and especially in Ithaca—deserve less. Deservingness has nothing to do with it. Rather, it is because I am trying to show that love has its costs.

Many of them tell me what they experienced was a spectacularly calm and destructively implosive pedagogical style. Some of them conveyed that they had not imagined as possible the way I interacted with their work, my multifaceted approaches to criticism, my mode of being in class. At least, they had not seen in such combination. It might have inspired some of them into actions that created problems for their long-term advisors and teachers. I really don't know.

So, what then were love's costs? For many years afterward, the institution (IRI at PUC-Rio) broke my heart by not asking me back.

Midway into my fifties, I learned I could still desire in ways that left me exposed and vulnerable. Perhaps it was my version of a mid-life crisis, evidenced not by ostentatious material acquisition or clandestine relationships but by a recommitment to a no-holds-barred pedagogical event when I knew damn well what I might be risking. So, yeah, I've said it. I've always known I worked on the sharp edge of risk, and not just in Rio. Do the right thing pedagogically and it can cost you your dream job.

* * *

Jesse Crane-Seeber loved to argue and debate as much as anyone I've met. He excelled at it. In an honors course, our arguments would sometimes become the show, and the rest of the students became interested spectators. It was both good theater and a clear expression of how to bring one's investments to the classroom.

We were discussing my claim that humanitarianism is a form of colonialism—an argument most of my students feared and rejected. I had built my prior life on such investments in humanitarian agendas until I read Michael Maren's *The Road to Hell* and Tzvetan Todorov's *The Conquest of America*. Both decisively demonstrate that military force and humanitarian aid are two arms of the same body.

Jesse was out of moves, exasperated, and defenseless. But he had one card still to play. With a snort and a roar, he shouted, "Well, fuck you then!"

The other students stopped breathing for a few beats, not knowing how I might combust. I held the moment. Delaying till the last possible instant, I laughed at maximum volume and said, "Well, that was some kind of fun."

When we later replicated the entire sequence a second time in the semester on a different topic, the other students were no less concerned for what Jesse's second "Fuck you!" might portend.

Jesse's memory differs a bit. He recalls storming out of class, and he reminds me that I later said to him, "That is when I knew I loved you."

* * *

Violet was one of four students from high-profile and well-funded programs at my college enrolled in my "Understanding Capitalism" course. She and two others dropped the course after I gave them comments that suggested how they might rewrite their papers. Violet stopped at my office and let me know exactly why she exited. She wanted me to know that she saw herself as an elite scholar. If professors like me treated her work with a "no grade," well, that only reflected the professor's incompetence. In addition, the word was out, she said, that I "taught to white students."

I understand her interpretation. I provide no extra support for students of color within the public circle of my classroom. Everyone is encouraged to express their views. If they mumble, hesitate, or cannot formulate their positions, I work with them to produce the articulation regardless of the student's political disposition. The result is that fascist, racist, sexist, and nationalist claims may get as much airtime as the opposite.

When I took my turn as chair of our department, I attended bi-weekly chairs meetings. One of the issues to emerge was what faculty should do when their students expressed racist and sexist comments. The head of our Center for the Study of Culture, Race and Ethnicity (CSCRE) immediately offered to hold workshops for faculty on how to fend off such comments. I raised my hand and expressed the following: "If I can get my students to say racist, sexist, and classist things, I consider that an achievement." I have no doubt that many of my colleagues were perplexed and distressed that a brown body and a founding member of the CSCRE could say such a thing.

* * *

Sabrina could ground a classroom around her profound silence. She watched everything and said nothing. Silent criticism radiated from her, and I could see how many of the other students absorbed this as a form of pressure. They needed her approval. I, too, found myself looking to her for either confirmation or disconfirmation. I still have no idea why some part of me wanted to please her.

Despite the sullen and powerful gravitas she carried, I was overjoyed when she finally arrived in my office.

She plopped down in my office, taking in a view of the lake. I opened cautiously with my usual lines: "How are you?" "How is your semester going?" and "How is our course going for you?" I paused attentively after each question waiting for a drip of information. She answered only my last question:

"I hate the course, and I hate you."

I'd heard such anger and violence from students before. Many times. But two elements of this delivery knocked me down: its unexpected arrival and a body language completely void of emotion.

I wanted to ask, "But why?!" Instead, I sat there, defeated.

* * *

I was a faculty panelist on a session dedicated to viewing and discussing a documentary film on *Sweet Honey in the Rock*, an activist musical group. When it came to my turn to speak, I confessed that I did not experience their music *as music*. I gave my reasons by laying out elements of my musical aesthetic and suggested that this African American band could be seen to participate not only in cultural appropriation but in forms of orientalism. Afterward, the dean who had put together the program and invited me to the panel thanked me privately for expressing some of her views and for provoking her thinking. But I suspect that she was also trying to balance the tongue-lashing I received from Elsie, a student in the audience who declared that she pitied someone whose pedantic posturing disallowed him to feel the power of great music. Earlier in the semester, she had interviewed me about enrolling in my "Cuba and Haiti" course. My course and I had not made the cut.

Her words hurt. The ease and confidence of this strike marks itself in my memory.

* * *

TB is one of my best friends. We are exercise partners, and he provides extra care for me when my health becomes tricky, and he is as warm and as loving a human being as any that walks this planet. He once invited me for a guest presentation in his class.

It became one of those magical occasions when everything seemed to fall in place. The room was small with a large table in the middle, no windows, and little space to stretch or move. I started in the Freirean style, a short introduction and then right to interaction with the students. I asked questions, I nudged, I poked, I paused, and I kept alert for bodily reactions in the back corners. Something in the air took control of us all: everyone spoke, they replied to each other's comments, and they rolled forward, unfolding their questions into ever deeper terrain.

I can convey such events with two analogies. In sports, sometimes your entire body comes into tune and suddenly everything is easy and perfect. When this happens to an entire team, it's as if it's a single organism in synch with itself. In West African music, the role of the master musician is minimal. Masters lead, of course, but they evoke and highlight elements that come from others to raise the sense of co-presence. For me, this is the apex of what can happen in a classroom. There is no better feeling.

But TB, it seemed, had been left out. After class, as we walked across campus, and as I was beaming at the miracle of it, he said, "You're a master-manipulator." I said nothing. The pain of that moment remains sharp. How does one speak when a stunning immanent process is assessed as a cunning external fraud? Fifteen years later, we are still friends, and we talk about everything but teaching.

* * *

I admired Sara-Maria Sorentino's work, but as it turns out, she didn't much care for mine. She was in my "Afghanistan and the Origins of Global Fury" course. She hardly said a word but produced only the most thoughtful and fully reasoned work. I believed that the course had gone well for us both. I was shocked then to hear her say, "I hated the course, and I hate you." Well, maybe those are not exactly her words, but you will not be surprised that I heard them as an echo of Sabrina's "I hate you."

Again, what struck me was the message's unexpectedness and deadpan delivery. Nevertheless, there is something about going through an experience a second time that allows you to clutch the ropes, smell the salts, gather your balance, and stand up straight, ready for another blow. I had a response: "Well, I certainly don't hate you, Sara-Maria."

Maybe that was enough for her to come back and allow us to work closely for years afterwards. I came to depend on her for curating my reading on pedagogy, race, and Lacanian interpretations of politics. Today, as a colleague, she challenges me at the center of my work.

Much of our bond, as I imagine it, results from our experience of her crisis after time spent as a researcher in Ghana. She had envisaged her relationship to Ghana as one between donor and receiver of knowledge and aid, but the elders of a particular village let her know that they had no need for her. Sara-Maria's paradigm collapsed, and it left her desperately searching for a different relationship. Upon her return, part of Sara-Maria's means of rebuilding herself and her relationship to Ghana was to read every book in my library. At a book or two a day, she had within months read most of the relevant material I put in her hands. This led her to larger libraries and the devouring of hundreds of books.

My associate dean believed that such voraciousness signaled deteriorating health and demanded that I stop feeding her addiction. When I refused, she made it clear that Sara-Maria's health at the college would be a part of my record. But Sara-Maria and I agreed that her reading was essential to her being. Disobeying my dean did not put my career in jeopardy. Nevertheless, the institution officially aligned itself against my best judgment. If only I would lecture and keep my distance.

* * *

Around 1999, a team of us had designed and then institutionalized the Center for the Study of Culture, Race, and Ethnicity. Over the years, we had hired a robust group of young faculty. Early on, the development team and the recent hires worked to understand each other. We met once a month, informally, for dinners and passionate debate over issues of race, gender, and representation.

It was during one of these dinners, held at a junior colleague's place, that I experienced what I might describe as a "second ambush." What differentiated the two is that in Syracuse for the team-teaching dinner at Lemon Grass, I was a junior colleague. Here, I was one of the seniors. My four young colleagues expressed their distress over my teaching—while my two senior colleagues took on an observer's role. One by one, they detailed how much of their time was devoted to putting back together students who had been undone by my courses and strategies. Their message to me was simple, clear, and united: We resent cleaning up your messes.

I suspect that they were surprised that I did not put up a fight. My single response was, "I won't defend myself." Sorayya was furious when I recounted the event. I was no less angry, but I also needed to think things through.

Months later, I had an answer for them, which, of course, was too late.

Frankey Johnson was one of those rare students who, from the start, looked for the meta processes of a classroom. She watched my teaching like a hawk, unsure if I could meet her high standards. Almost every day after class, she would assess and critique my teaching decisions. Mostly, I listened; I did not defend, except with my smile. One day, in class, another student named Kourtney and I had a risky and flagrant encounter. These often appear with students who have taken multiple classes with me. It's when I betray their trust, the *Whiplash* (2014) moment. The instance, that is, when I know I am likely to lose them, at least in the short term and, perhaps, altogether. Kourtney stormed out of class—a reaction that I anticipated. Frankey stared in disbelief as I let her go without comment, without regret, and without apology.

Later in my office, Frankey counseled me sternly: "You need to reach out to her because otherwise she's not coming back." I held firm. Three weeks went by, and Frankey continued prompting me about Kourtney. Finally, I turned to Frankey and said, "The message I am sending, Kourtney, is that I have faith she can sort this out without me. If I hover, I undermine her conviction that I believe in her."

Frankey still believes I miscalculated.

* * *

For many years, Ron Denson and I took turns convening the "Junior Honors Seminar." I treasured it because, in my role as convener, I had the opportunity to select four other professors who were responsible for two-week teaching units on a topic of their choice. It was a rare chance to learn something outside of my usual horizon. I loved the pedagogical tension caused by having two professors in the room whose authority might clash. The course was like going back to school for me, and it gave me a sense of what teaching meant to my colleagues.

I tried to recruit teachers from the "hard" sciences—college departments furthest from my comfort zone, but that was not always possible.

Like the students, my colleagues generally had not been in a classroom with two teachers. Most of them were discomfited when I tried to create cross-authority tensions. Still, some relished the scene. Indeed, Catherine Taylor, a theorist from the writing department, turned the tables on me. She required students to do in-class writing according to very specific prompts.

My body resisted her imperative for us to write, I found her prompts too restrictive, and I wanted to rebel right there, right then. I was back in school and did not like it. It took me a second semester before I could accept that I needed what she was offering. Namely, that writing presents folded emotion as an object outside of us, something with which we can play and unfold that does not immediately merge the writer and the writing.

* * *

Jerry was a business school student in my "Understanding Capitalism" course. He was articulate, loved to speak, and had plenty to say—a pontificator. "You're a natural professor," I teased him. But soon I realized that I could not get him to share the floor. His voice monopolized the classroom.

After private discussions had no effect, I went public. I wrote his name on the board and placed three square boxes next to it. "That is how many times you get to speak in class." Each time he spoke, I checked a box. He tested me, of course. The next day, I gave him two boxes and then one. Finally, four days later, I asked him not to speak at all unless he could convince one of his classmates to give up their turn to him. He was maddened and defiant. He made a long speech indicating how my conduct was unprofessional and outrageous.

* * *

Alex is one of my self-declared working-class students. She is a rarity in two ways: she is somehow managing to attend our expensive private college, and she admits to a sense of deprivation compared to her classmates. Equally important, she is open about the sexual abuse she suffered. She is willing to talk about anything but only on the stipulation that my office door is left open. I assured her that I had the same requirement for my office hours.

She had not been by in a year or two—having given up on my teaching. She eventually reconsidered and stopped in. We were catching up, and she was sharing additional dimensions of her pain when my colleague across the hall got up, walked across the waiting room, and gently closed my door. Alex re-opened it immediately in a near panic. The professor reprimanded us. It was inappropriate, she said, to discuss such intimate details so openly, so loudly, and with the door open so wide. We waited as she walked back to her office and shut her door, then we laughed.

CHAPTER 6

Musical Metaphors[1]
and Learning from Students

I was a little anxious as I sat with my spouse waiting for Oliver Mtuku-dzi to open his set. "Tuku," as he is known, is one of the great voices of our world. His performances, which include dancing as well as sing-ing, deliver a cascade of energy that can electrify and overwhelm his audience. I hoped that he would match his performance years ago that many of us experienced as among the best heard at our local venue, the Finger Lakes GrassRoots Festival. Today, however, the band was down to a quartet, and Tuku's mood was somber. A few songs in, he shared that his son had died a mere six months ago.

I didn't hear much happening in the first three pieces of Tuku's set. Still, the audience stayed. His quiet self-assurance projected a warm indifference, as if he were saying, "Just take in what you need." And soon, it was all enchantment.

What happened? Here's the most succinct way I have of putting it: He trusted his audience. He was confident in the possibility of the mo-ment. He displayed, I might say, an aesthetics of emergence.

Some years prior, at the same festival, I had heard Tuku's compa-triot, the great Thomas Mapfumo, whom I love even more. Mapfumo lacks Tuku's world-class sonority, but he vocalizes a hollowness that draws you into its center as if he is seeking to quench his thirst through an ancient well.

Mapfumo's band is built around two mbira players who laid down deep, tension-filled grooves. Mapfumo did not dance, jump, or call out

---

1. Parts of this chapter have appeared as "Absent Any Spectacle: an aesthetics of emergence," *Millennium: Journal of International Studies*, 49 (3) pp. 617–619, November 2021.

to his audience. Indeed, he sometimes sat down to sing. And yet, my body was tethered to his will.

It was the last set of the night, and for the ride home, I tried to puzzle out how he had managed to hold me so totally, so effortlessly.

I can tell you what he didn't do, and it was the same things that Tuku didn't do:

- no call outs,
- no shout outs,
- no slow build to an emotional and technical apex,
- no dancers,
- no video,
- no call-and-response with the audience,
- no begging the audience to wave, or jump, or dance, or shout, or sing,
- no audacious chops or blistering licks,
- no vocal gymnastics,
- no desire to let you bathe in his velvety, jagged tenor,
- no stretching the pace beyond the present moment,
- no gesture towards easy feelings, and
- no effort to build a fleeting solidarity.

What's left when you remove the tricks? That's what I want to know.

* * *

Cut to Islamabad, sometime in the 1980s. I was on summer break from the university and visiting my parents' house. We had to be creative in this dead-end town because it had one cinema, one TV station, and nothing ever happened.

But on that day, I needed only to iron my clothes because I had secured my father's invitation for a sitar concert. *Never mind*, I said to myself, *that it's a US Embassy function*. Never mind that the sitar player is white. At worst, I could pass the evening silently mocking the event. When the show was about to start, my expectations decreased further when the sitarist appeared wearing an ill-fitting kurta—very tall, very thin, and very, very pale.

Within a few notes of the *alap*, I was in his spell. I began estimating his years of training. I did not doubt he was a better Pakistani than me, and I chastised myself for my presumptions. Then I turned off my critic's ear, closed my eyes, and let him take me.

* * *

For all my courses, I get to my classroom ten minutes early so I can access my music library and have tunes playing as students arrive. I know from years of teaching experience that students engage music via habitual gateways. Some require vocals, others need lyrics, while others are inattentive without guitar or horn solos. These entry ports favor melody and harmony over rhythm and percussion—Europe over Africa. This means that they cannot hear the small percussion instruments that create the backbone of much African and African-derived music.

I compensate with my musical selections. During the semester, I saturate them with small and big percussion, and I avoid easily understood lyrical content, which means I offer only non-English vocals. I soak their ears with immanent instead of transcendent solos, and occasionally, I play atonal and arrhythmic pieces. I don't explain or discuss the music. I wait instead for that delicious moment when they ask, "What *is* that?" Fishing takes patience, but patience is itself the catch.

* * *

Music has stealth. It slips in under our radar and scatters our biases. It subdues us to surrender, lifts our spirits, and allows us to commune with beings beyond ourselves. Yet, these qualities do not merely linger above the Earth like a cloud. Music's capacity to enrapture derives from specific cultural soils: musicians make music in a specific time and in historically and culturally shaped spaces. Musicians solve immediate problems, articulate particular feelings, create sonic utopias, expose hidden fears, and formulate tangible dreams.

Cultural musical forms have an existence apart from their commercial consumption; they do not simply appear like tubs of ice cream displayed in the frozen section of the supermarket. In fact, difference implies critique. *Always.* This is so whether we speak of different ice cream, different cultures, or different musical forms. Thus, pistachio is not *merely* sitting next to the mocha fudge offering us different tastes for different days. They converse in critique. The pistachio challenges the mocha fudge. It rebukes the deep-bass flavors of the chocolate accents and the bittersweet-coffee flavor. These flavors, says the pistachio, are too deep, too complicated, too heavy for ice cream's essentially playful nature. Meanwhile, the mocha fudge reproaches the simplicity and lightness of pistachio as being close to the plain nothingness of vanilla. The mocha fudge declares that pistachio is not sufficiently robust to satisfy the deeper human needs that real ice cream fulfills.

I want to suggest that each of the musical forms we study can also be seen as a critique of all other musical forms, including our favorites. What do our musical tastes mean? How do these tastes ground our identity as aesthetic and political beings?

* * *

Then there is the further issue of North American students not just consuming but also producing music that emerges from other locales. Are they aware of this music's political, cultural, or spiritual nature? Would they consume and produce it in the same way if we had a better knowledge and appreciation of its deeper purposes? Having understood this music's context, how can we produce a meaningful posture towards it? Does the fullness of this music speak to the lack of something in our own musical traditions? Does identifying the similarities and differences in our relative aesthetic and political postures help us reconstruct our own lives?

* * *

My former student Amy Senior told me after years of traveling in the African continent that outside of Nigeria and Ghana, it is Celine Dion who reigns over the musical airwaves.

US culture dominates the world, especially sound streams. Global music sales are determined mostly by the demand of teenagers in the United States and Europe. This means that Western popular music saturates musical cultures in South America, Africa, and Asia. Moreover, it means that local cultures, instead of cultivating their own rich musical traditions, switch to western popular musical styles. Is this not a dire cultural emergency? Is not musical diversity under a greater threat than tropical rain forests?

Western cultural (including music) and economic power work as structures of imperialism that dominate other parts of the world. You and I participate in this cultural imperialism without knowing it. My music courses aim to put cultural diversity in students' ears by offering music from Ghana, Nigeria, India, Pakistan, and Brazil, but such sonic offerings do not change listening routines. These habits are grounded in acts of devotion to family members, to intense memories, and to secret nationalisms.

Please know that I have never *not* been subject to cultural imperialism. My shift in understanding diverse perspectives was the result of noting that it was musicians who deciphered the problem of cultural imperialism. This meant a shift in emphasizing not politics but art and aesthetics as the key to developing perspective. As with art, so also with pedagogy: the best route is long and indirect, the orbit and not the vector.

* * *

South Asian raags can last 30 to 120 minutes. In comparison, Brazilian songs last from two to five minutes. Students in my music classes can develop the patience required for Fela Kuti's twelve- to twenty-minute songs, but the duration and form of raags demand too much. For example, I took my students to a concert by the explosive sarod duo of Amaan Ali Bangash and Ayaan Ali Bangash. Some fell asleep, and others told me that they couldn't tell when the concert started because the musicians seemed to be tuning for the full two hours. Western limitations in apprehending non-Western music can work both ways. At a music festival in 1971, Ravi Shankar's ensemble was tuning instruments getting ready to perform. The audience broke out in applause at the end of their tuning. Ravi Shankar addressed the audience: "Thank you, if you appreciate the tuning so much, I hope you will enjoy the playing more." Pedagogies of tuning seem untroubled about the boundaries between the event, its prelude, and its sequel.[2] Indeed, the meaning of an event may not arrive until years later.

---

2. With thanks to Richa Nagar for this point.

In the mid-seventies, I saw Miles Davis' band at Stables, a club in East Lansing, Michigan, when he was near the end of his electric phase. They played for five minutes before some minor snafu triggered Miles' temper, and he walked off. Police cleared the venue for the second show in which Miles played for three hours. But my five minutes—I still savor them.

As a compromise, to accommodate my students' attention span, I found a nine-minute version of raag "Chandrakauns" by the great vocalist Salamat Ali Khan. The first time I played it, Katerina Leinhart put her head down on her desktop, enveloped herself with her arms, and cried. I noted it with some curiosity. Years later, Maggie Kelly had the same response to this piece, but without Katerina's wish for enclosure. Sorayya reminded me that our friend, Laura McNeal, cried when hearing Ajoy Chakrabarty's pathos-inducing vocals one night in Syracuse.

* * *

I had long assumed that only South Asians had the cultural resources to be so deeply touched by *pukka raag* (full raag). In college, my jazz-head friends could swing and sway to the bird calls and sonic torturing of abstract jazz but had nothing kind to say about classical South Asian vocals. Somehow, though, Salamat Ali Khan and Ajoy Chakrabarty cut through our cultural fog while directly filling Katerina, Kelly, and Laura with a kind of joy. What had I underestimated?

* * *

I pleaded with the assistant provost, Dr. Tanya Saunders, to include me on the organizing committee when she announced plans for concerts and lectures on the music of the African Diaspora. During our year of planning, Dr. Saunders hinted that teaching a course on the music of the African Diaspora might be a good way to complement the series. My ears did not register her first five requests because I assumed she was calling on the music faculty, the other five that constituted our committee.

A few months later, I surmised that there would be no response unless it was mine. But now I faced a sobering challenge summarized by the following Fleetwood Mac lyrics: "I can't help about the shape I'm in/ I can't sing, I ain't pretty and my legs are thin." That is, I don't play an instrument, I can't read music, and I have never had any musical training.

To decrease my anxiety, I sat in on my friend Steve Pond's "Survey of Jazz" course at Cornell. Initially, that was a mistake because I was so out of my element. Steve spent most of his life singing in a choir, dancing, and drumming in a jazz band. Academia was a mid-life calling. As I witnessed Steve dance, sing, and lecture, I thought, *It would take me more than one lifetime to acquire a fraction of his skills.*

Despite my acute apprehension, I offered the course the following semester with the help of my pro bono teaching assistant, John Dobry. As we proceeded, I beamed at what I thought was a perfectly balanced encounter; my students could not doubt that I was learning from them. Nevertheless, I continued to project my angst about whether I could claim the role of teacher.

At the mid-semester mark, Kara Pangburn stormed into my office. Kara played the French horn but gave it up upon arriving at Ithaca College. She was weeks away from graduation and suddenly deeply invested in the course. Here are her exact words: "This course is too important for me to have you fuck it up. You need to get out of our way and let us do the work." Her face was so red, her engagement so evident, that I sat there admiring her resolve and marveled that a student was yelling at me for getting in the way of her learning. Imagine.

* * *

I am offering the first iteration of the music course, officially titled "The Political Economy of African Diaspora Music." John gave me courage as the course proceeded. When, in the seventh week, we turned to reggae, I was startled by the rebellion brewing in the class.

Andrew Sacks was captain of the football team and student body president. Sal Belia was his teammate and brother in arms. They occupied the middle of the room. Andrew raised his hand and declared, "You can give me any fucking grade you want on my paper, but I am not analyzing Bob Marley's music." Sal nodded vigorously.

"You feel the same way, Sal?" I asked.

"Yeah, yeah, I'm not messing with Bob."

I replay that moment in slow motion, as if I am Neo in *The Matrix*. I turn it, ponder it, and enjoy it. I had stumbled onto something precious.

Over the years, students persisted in challenging the premise of critical examination. Still, it took me many years to excavate the meaning of those moments. When I read Timothy Brennan's pivotal book, *Secular Devotion: Afro-Latin Music and Imperial Jazz*,[3] I finally guessed at what had blocked Andrew and Sal. The simple version of Brennan's argument is that we still practice religious spirituality, but today, music is the object of our veneration. I've never thanked Andrew and Sal (or Malikah and Matt, see later in this chapter) for triggering my thinking on the role of the sacred in this planet's musical life.

My music course entices students until they confront the dangers of knowing: Does knowledge destroy or enhance the sacred? I began to understand their reluctance.[4]

* * *

James Searl was also a student in the first of my music courses. As a practicing bassist, he was puzzling out a different problem. Hailing from Rochester, New York, he was a serious critical thinker fully devoted to reggae. Bassists seem to gravitate to my methods, which I don't think is accidental, as they are subject to the ensemble in their own practice. James took lessons from another white reggae bassist called "Solid." Solid insisted that music did not belong to anyone and, therefore, James needn't worry about cultural appropriation or cultural imperialism.

James was going to devote his life to reggae, there was no question about it. What remained was what posture he and his band, Giant Panda Guerilla Dub Squad, would take towards Jamaica's cultural, traditional, and musical genealogy. It was not a life-or-death matter for James, but it was close.

* * *

James Napoli was another pro bono teaching assistant and the most unassuming person I've ever met. His parents had raised him on funds

---

3. Verso, 2008.

4. "All changes in deeply held beliefs involve an experience of loss or mourning. If . . . teachers are to help in this activity of changing deeply invested feelings, they would do well to understand the mourning process." Alcorn, Marshall. (2002). *Changing the Subject in English Class* (Carbondale: Southern Illinois University Press), p. 111.

they secured making and selling tie-dye shirts at music festivals. James was ever-present but quiet. To compensate for his shyness, we decided that he would have full class periods to teach uninterrupted.

James made a seventy-five-minute presentation that I recall as the highlight of that semester. Using not only wide-ranging musical samples but also illustrations from drama, literature, jokes, and the philosophy of Aristotle, James argued that much of the Western aesthetic tends to be developmentally linear with a clear apex and a short denouement. In contrast, the aesthetic sensibility from other parts of the world tended to be circular, often without an identifiable opening or closing. Not the "one" followed by "two, three, and four" but rhythmic circularity in which others can enter and exit at will.

His musical example for circularity was the reggae band *Midnite*'s "The Foolish and the Wise." He drew a large circle on the board, and with each repetition of the musical pattern, he filled in the part each instrument played within the circle. As he completed the circle, with the class spellbound, he suggested that the circular aesthetic was closer to the worldview of Buddhism and Hinduism.

What compelled us in his presentation was not just the poised precision and interweaving of various threads beyond music. It was also the serene joy with which James presented the material, offering it in a playful and lighthearted manner. Still, we understood the profundity of his analysis. One underestimates students at one's own peril, a lesson that, somehow, I must relearn every week.

* * *

A year later, I offer a second iteration of my music class. Andrew Battles is my pro bono teaching assistant this time. We are in the music school's finest space, a state-of-the-art room with acoustic design, two pianos, and a powerful sound system. Somehow, the conservatory's administration has overlooked their implicit rule forbidding entry into their premises to non-music professors. The only problem is that the seats are fixed, so it is impossible to sit in a circle.

Andrew is a student at the music school as well as the bassist for the jazz band Reichlin/Battles/Dobry (RBD). I attend all their performances. Andrew is in front of the class explaining that West African musicians do not necessarily orient themselves around the "one." Everyone nods, but I haven't a clue. I raise my hand from the back and ask, "The one?" Andrew doesn't understand my question. I clarify: "What do you mean by 'the one'?" Andrew stops what he has prepared. His wry smile lets me know that I am in for a treat.

He plays something (I wish I could recall what) and asks the class to point to the sky each time "the one" arrives. Every few beats, in unison, the entire class points their index finger to the sky. I am stupefied. He plays a different cut, then a third and fourth. Each time the students locate "the one" without trying. Their bodies just know where it is. I am not embarrassed by my lack of basic knowledge. Rather, I am amazed that I did not know their secret language after a lifetime of listening to thousands of songs on records, tapes, reel-to-reel, and compact discs.

For months, I practice finding "the one," pointing to the sky every time I hear it. Sorayya indulges me but worries about my divided attention when we drive. So, instead, I tap the steering wheel or slap my thigh.

Andrew is not done with me once he realizes the range of my technical ignorance. Lesson two is finding the clave rhythm. He plays something by Fela Kuti, Sunny Adé, or Chucho Valdés and turns the attention of the class to me. "Hey Naeem, can you find the clave?" I worked at it.

I raise the courage to make a small presentation following Michael Veal's explanation[5] of how Fela's compositions create a cross-rhythmic tension by transferring the role of traditional drums to the alto, tenor, and bass guitars. Andrew gently stops me in the middle and suggests that I had confused the tenor guitar for the alto guitar. I stop immediately and retreat, swallowing my pride. It was many iterations of the course before I would try another presentation.

* * *

Phil Weinrobe was yet another one of my pro bono teaching assistants—another bassist but also a composer and bandleader. His written work in my courses was superb. When I introduced him to my class, I decided to call him "Master Phil," and I asked the students to do the same, reasoning that if he was my master, then he could be theirs too. His housemate refused the hierarchy. Instantly, another student

---

5. Veal, Michael. (2000). *Fela* (Philadelphia: Temple University Press).

responded, "If some won't call him Master Phil, I'll call him, Master-Master Phil." From then on, he has been "Master-Master Phil."

Phil went on to lead several bands in and around Ithaca, and he currently owns and operates a music studio in New York City. We wrote a paper together, "A Medium of Others: Rhythmic Soundscapes as Critical Utopias."[6] He wrote all the technical materials but also some of the theoretical elements. Here, too, I was his apprentice.

* * *

Like me, Malikah Waajid had no technical musical skills. She insisted, nevertheless, that this music belonged to her and to her people. African-derived music was a part of her heritage. She shared that her grandmother sang her songs while she rocked Malikah. A revered memory.

Malikah vehemently objected to our "dissection" of her music. We were killing something that was living, breathing, and sacred. We were violating her culture.

My heart skipped a beat.

How was I going to get out of this? She was challenging the very existence of my course, questioning my right to offer it, and undermining a premise that I did not know I held until she negated it, namely, that our technical "dissection" enhanced rather than demeaned the music, the culture, and its history.

Breathe.

Build on the rift, I implored myself. I listened, I absorbed, I resisted the urge to defend. Minutes went by but so slowly.

From within that silence, Matt Bozzone's hand shot up. The six-foot-five guard for the basketball team turned to Malikah and said: "I have been playing jazz drums since I was ten. Do you believe that my decade-long engagement with your culture counts for nothing?"

* * *

The film *Whiplash* (2014) went by in a flash for me. I immediately asked students of my "Writing and Criticism" class to view it. The

---

6. In M. I. Franklin (ed) *Resounding International Relations: On Music, Culture and Politics,* Palgrave, 2005.

Table 6.1.

	High theoretical application	Low theoretical application
High need to be liked	(Rare)	Most teachers
Low need to be liked	(The ideal)	Fletcher

film explores the relationship between a jazz band teacher, Terence Fletcher, and a super-ambitious student drummer, Andrew Neiman. While both are developed characters, they are stretched to the extreme.

Andrew aims to become a great drummer—the next Elvin Jones, let's say. He announces at a family dinner that if he is broke, drunk, and a heroin addict at age thirty-four, as was Charlie Parker, he will accept those terms if his name lives on as a great artist. Fletcher learns of Andrew's skills and summons him to be his student.

While both characters fascinate me, my focus is Fletcher because he possesses tools I lack. He doesn't seem to care about his students' feelings. Specifically, he doesn't care if they despise him. He bullies them with angry rants that are sexist, anti-Semitic, homophobic, and ageist. These histrionics are designed to reduce his students to tears and to quit his band altogether. He even bullies them physically, slapping them if he believes the teaching moment calls for it. He gets away with the abuse because he produces results, such as prizes at competitions for his bands and jobs for his graduates. Fletcher is driven to produce greatness in his students. He believes that anything less than his fascistic methods will deprive the world of the next Charlie Parker or Louis Armstrong.

I deplore all this, even as I accept the film's premises and respect it as a thought experiment. In addition, I am stirred by what Fletcher makes me realize.

Imagine a two-by-two box[7] where the rows are "high" and "low" on the dimension "theoretical application to teaching." The columns are "high" and "low" in the dimension of "need to be liked by students." This gives us four boxes: most professors fit into the overlap of "low theoretical application" and "high need to be liked." My sample for this observation includes my own teachers, and it includes colleagues I have observed either while co-teaching or while assessing them for perfor-

---

7. With thanks to Patrick Jackson and, before him, James Caporaso.

mance reviews. It is rare to find teachers who show a "high theoretical application" and also a " high need to be liked," but I have met a few. This segment is not a dead-end by any means, but its limitations are immediate. That is, making the right pedagogic move can be hijacked by the desire to be well thought of by students and colleagues alike.

This leaves two segments. The one occupied by Fletcher is the cross between "low theoretical application" and "low need to be liked."[8] Drill sergeants, sports coaches, and curmudgeons occupy this space. The fourth segment is my ideal: "high theoretical application" with "low need to be liked." Nevertheless, those aspiring for such an ideal can learn something from the space Fletcher occupies. Namely, how does one best approach pedagogical astuteness *without* becoming a monster?

When I need to be monstrous in the eyes of my students, I play the role. For example, I have told students that they can no longer enroll in my classes. I have performed the part of a "Third World revolutionary," knowing that perhaps something in my students' image of me would break if I let them see me as such. I deliberately aim to quash their desire to hold on to their innocence, their optimism, and their heroism. In every case, however, I also explain my reasoning.

Does my wish to explain my reasoning expose my desire to be liked, if by no one else, then at least in my own eyes? I abhor Fletcher's contempt for his students, but I am attracted to his clarity.

* * *

Baruch Whitehead is tall, large, and bespectacled with a generous smile and a kind face. He was the only black professor in the music school. We both taught versions of "Worlds of Music" and agreed to offer it together. He has all the skills I do not: he can sing, dance, read music, play the piano, and most importantly, he can turn a random assortment of students into singing groups and percussion ensembles. I sat in on his African drumming course during a sabbatical. He trusted me to be the sole percussionist at a short gig in front of the Park School.

---

8. Emma Kast offers a different take: "I interpret Fletcher's method as having a rather high theoretical application, however barbaric. The difference is that you do not have a stake in the student's career outcome (at least you perform not having a stake), whereas Fletcher makes it clear that the student will deeply disappoint him if s/he is not the next Charlie Parker."

This was my first and last public music performance—a momentous experience that I am trying somehow to import into my curriculum vitae. My gratitude to Baruch is boundless. I think of him as a superhero who survives the strictures of the European vault we call the music school. I hope he considers me as a brother of sorts, not a black brother, but an Asian brother, perhaps.

As we worked on our co-teaching, we encountered a glitch that I could not overcome. Baruch comes from the gospel tradition of black churches, so his primary medium is harmony. And yet, his yearly summer trips with students to Ghana have brought out his percussive and rhythmic heritage.

In class, he talked about what a return to the "motherland" meant for him. Often, he was nearly in tears as he spoke about his visits to Ghana, but a part of me hears his travel stories as patronizing. He speaks, for example, of "our responsibility" for alleviating their poverty, illiteracy, and lack of education. In class, his passion is so contagious that I let it go, especially since no less a giant than W. E. B. Du Bois does the same.[9] But Tarisai Gombe was not impressed and did not let it go. She called him out point-blank: "We are Africans, you are an American, your homeland is right here. We don't need you." Harsh, even by my standards, but I understood her anger.

In private, though, I was stuck. "Baruch," I said, "I can't have you talking about Ghana and Ghanaians in terms that suggest that they need our help. Aren't we trying to learn their music because West Africans are the greatest percussive masters the world has ever known?"

I was playing my usual Third World role, a role for which I had practiced my entire life. He looked at me with sincere confusion, "But don't they need our help? Are we not responsible for our brothers and sisters?" I responded, "Yes, of course, but that is a long and complicated conversation." The boundary was revealed, but neither of us knew how to bridge it.[10]

* * *

9. See, for example, his "The Hands of Ethiopia," in Du Bois (1999 [1920]), Darkwater: Voices from Within the Veil (New York: Dover).

10. In recent correspondence, Baruch Whitehead writes that he has "evolved" into a different understanding of these issues. We might still build that bridge as I, too, have changed as a teacher and colleague.

In the fall of 2009, in perhaps the tenth version of my music course, I hadn't found a volunteer to be my teaching assistant. I was going it alone in early September, having presented seven of the eight characteristics[11] of West African music:

- Call-and-Response
- Heterogeneous Sound Ideal (Plurality of Timbres)
- Percussive Manner of Playing all Instruments Including Voice
- High-Density Musical Events
- Integration of Listener Response (Dance)
- Technical and Expressive Restraint
- Aesthetics of Imperfection

As the period ended, I told them that the seventh, namely "rhythmic tension" or "polyrhythmic clash," was the most difficult for me to explain because of my lack of musical training. I told them I would try to cover this seventh characteristic in our next meeting, but I worried that I wouldn't be able to demonstrate this crucial element and might call on them for help.

As I was walking out of the Music building, Heather Rosner was walking in. We knew each other through Professor Whitehead, with whom she had traveled to Ghana to learn drumming and dancing. We stopped to chat. I asked her if she would demonstrate "rhythmic tension" for my class. She arrived with two djembes and cowbells for the students. Her fifteen-minute demonstration captivated us all. As she was packing up her instruments, I asked her if she didn't mind staying for the full period. She smiled and stayed. As she exhibited various aspects of West African drumming, it became clear to me that Heather possessed two crucial components of what I call "deep teaching": a saturated passion for the activity/ideas being taught and acute listening skills.

Heather started visiting our class once a week. She brought the instruments and then organized us into a singing, drumming, and dancing ensemble. We even put on a concert at the end of the semester. We had only one number in our repertoire, so for our encore, we performed it again.

---

11. Olly Wilson presents six of these in his "Black Music as an Art Form," (1983); the rest are my extrapolations.

CHAPTER 7

From Theory to Healing[1]

I access Steve Reich's minimalist and repetitive music via two metaphors. First, waves materialize in a foreground that recede into the background as new waves emerge to claim the foreground. Second, his cross-beat cycles between synchrony and asynchrony, like the two clocks in my first-year dorm room.

I have the same two relationships with my field, international relations theory. Today, political economy is coming into vogue, but when I entered the field as a professional, I had to hide and then translate my orientation toward political economy. Likewise, whereas from the 1990s onward I was discouraged from thinking about teaching, suddenly my field has discovered pedagogy.

Last year's International Studies Association (ISA) annual meeting had multiple pedagogy panels. I have been a dutiful attendee since 1987 and do not recall such interest in previous decades. Because the universe is curved, what was in front now appears behind and what was behind is now something we can catch up to.

Andy Paras, Patrick Jackson, and Jamie Frueh, among others, are at the forefront of this interest in pedagogy. The panels organized by Andy and Patrick are particularly demanding, as they require reading a book, writing a five-page comment on it, and then reading the comments of all the other panelists. Patrick and Andy required us to read books by Parker Palmer at the last two ISAs. An adaption of what I wrote for their panel follows.

---

1. Parts of this chapter appeared in "Pupils Dilated: Towards a Pedagogy of Emergence," Kate Schick and Claire Timperley (eds) *Subversive Pedagogies: Radical Possibility in the Academy*, (Routledge, 2022) pp. 81–91.

The first time through Parker J. Palmer's *To Know as We are Known: Education as a Spiritual Journey* (1993),[2] I was annoyed by his piety. He battered me with his "musts" and "oughts" (p. 8). His Christianity, I thought, was symptomatic of his urgency, of his desire to teach me something.

But there was also much to like. I was compelled to return, even though I did not want to. I was more relaxed the second time, probably because I had already registered my complaints. Before I get to the benefits of Palmer's book, I want to express its limitations in one sentence: Palmer's spiritual approach is nested neither in a political economy nor in a political psychology.

What makes this book so appealing is that it makes me feel less alone. There are only two colleagues in my teaching career with whom I would dare utter the following words: "We teach with love." I have dreaded this phrase as expressing something Hallmark-like. And, I have feared that love in the classroom is a taboo topic. But Palmer is clear that the love he examines and promotes is rigorous and demanding (pp. 9, 46). It is more like fire than like chocolate. I am moved by his question, "How can the places where we learn to know become places we learn to love?" (p. 9).

Palmer overlooks, nevertheless, that love, besides being a solution to the problem of an overly objectivist pedagogy, is also a problem. Love of routine, love of slavishness, love of the source of our affection—family, friends, nation. Such love prevents students from moving into a community of knowing.

Love is Janus-faced. One side can create a rigorous learning community that demands deep listening. The other side comforts us when we ignore or bypass critical knowledge. Some call this aspect of love reification, or dogma, or socialization. Others call it family life. Whatever we call it, this love is sticky, as the Lacanians might say. This love can keep us from greater curiosity and sharper truths. As Palmer observes, "We find it safer to seek facts that keep us in power rather than truths that require us to submit" (p. 40).

Palmer bypasses the magnitude of this problem by asking, why do we choose the lazy pedagogy? (p. 39). Why do we act against our bet-

---

2. Palmer, Parker. (1993). *To Know as We are Known: Education as a Spiritual Journey* (New York: Harper Collins).

ter selves? These are excellent questions, but instead of lingering with them, Palmer's perfunctory answers reveal his lack of commitment to the questions themselves. Sometimes, we find the right vein, but we don't have the patience to mine it.

A second problem is Palmer's emphasis on consensus, harmony, and reconciliation (p. 111). While he is excellent on the centrality of tension and paradox (pp. 104, 111), he wants to resolve, not cultivate, the kind of tension that promotes a dissensus. Again, on display is an unwillingness to linger.

Palmer's most serious flaw is his desire to believe that he can still be the good teacher, the good person, the good Christian. In a world that is structurally tainted, this posture betrays the hopes he espouses. Even the teacher who lives up to Palmer's highest ideals must still implement the kind of love that students will inevitably experience as loss and violence, at least at first. Learning is a kind of ferocity against a prior self, and Palmer naively believes that he can find a way around this rupture.

Still, there are so many gems, a bounty I want to list.

- His emphasis on healing the world (p. 8);
- The powerful work he derives from the monastic tradition that gives us the reading of texts as a kind of sacred activity, the practice of reading and thinking as a kind of prayer, and the goal of creating communities of learning (p. 17);
- The link in all epistemological chains are not ideas and theories but rather a teacher, a mentor, a guide (p. 29);
- The foundational unit of teaching, learning, and knowing is relationship (p. 53);
- The essential relationship of "truth" to "troth" is a kind of fidelity and faithfulness (p. 31);
- In knowing the world, we are also coming to be known by it (p. 36);
- Learning is about transformation while not-learning is about the fear of transformation (p. 54);
- We cannot learn without being in love (p. 58);
- As we read texts, they also read us (pp. 59, 62);
- The classroom is, in fact, necessarily within the world (p. 88); and,
- We cannot begin to know ourselves without knowing the Hitler within us (p. 102).

As I immerse myself in these claims, ideas, and practices, reading them on Palmer's pages makes me less alone. It affirms that rather than being randomly wild in my pedagogical trajectory, my path has not been unsystematic.

* * *

At last year's ISA (2021), Andy Paras and Patrick Jackson had us read Palmer's earlier work *To Know as We are Known* (1993), which I liked a bit better than *The Courage to Teach* (1998). Both books irritate me even as I find them appealing. *Courage*, more than *To Know*, has a preachy sales-pitch undertone that had me wishing for more storytelling and less propounding of principles. Still, every ten pages or so, I noted something I wanted to keep as a reminder. For example, I like Palmer's emphasis on wholeness (p. 4) and on what certain types of Marxists and Hegelians might call "expressive holism" (p. 122). I second his call that we recognize teachers' vulnerabilities (p. 17), and I agree that academics hurt themselves when we distrust what he calls "personal truths." I enjoy his criticism that we are, in fact, "blaming the victims" (p. 41) when we complain about our students. He affirms my experience that nearly all pedagogic conversation devolves into "technique talk" (p. 145). I confirm his claims that the power of the "sacred" is in play in the classroom (p. 111) and that truth is not attained via democratic processes (p. 92). His diagnosis that teachers need to be liked is a crucial problem (p. 49) and central to my own vision of reforming teaching. Finally, I love his language when he asks how long we should wait before we "smite" students for uttering statements that are totally false or utterly offensive (p. 134). The subtext here is that we should wait a very long time, perhaps forever, before reproaching students with our power, knowledge, and skill.

I love, most of all, two passages that produce vital questions. One solves my problem about what to do with student praise. Usually, I say, "But I didn't do anything. You did all the work." What I will now say is, "What is it about *you* that allowed . . . [my] mentoring to happen?" (p. 21). The second passage possesses a Hegelian/Lacanian question that teachers almost never ask (p. 139): What need in teachers do students fill?

To Know also hides elements that need exposure. If we think of the medium as painting, then Palmer paints in bright colors or in pastels, and his strokes are impressionistic. Too much so. Missing are the darker hues and those quiet waves of understanding that come only when we are drowned in a sense of resignation. I need less Gustav Klimt and more Mark Rothko.

Palmer's two books are too internalized for me (p. 20). They are absent both the macro-structures of political economy and the microstructures of (Freudian) psychology. As a result, he does not have a strong enough response to the charge that when we practice his methods, we are "doing therapy" (p. 64). A better response might be that what we do is both different from and better than therapy because, instead of severing them from each other, we expose how dynamic micro-structures are dynamic macro-structures. It is this severing that causes therapy's ultimate failure.

While Palmer is insightful about the role of organizations, namely that they "represent the principle of order and conservation . . . [and] . . . they are the vessels in which society holds hard won treasures from the past" (p. 164), he misses that they also contain an active denial of genocide, slavery, sexism, and war crimes—what Adorno calls "barbarism." In sum, I might say that while Palmer briefly addresses pessimism, he does not consider the difference between pessimism and resignation and, therefore, is unaware of the tremendous energy resignation releases. As I like to say in my classes, capitulation is 90 percent of victory.

Sadly, Palmer produces the condition he fears, namely, that he is peddling "false hope about the renewal of teaching and learning" (p. 164).

Can we find a better analysis?

* * *

Hannah Britton could not believe that her professor confessed an inability to read poetry. "But it's easier than reading Hegel and Marx," she said. "All you have to do is pay attention." I had incorporated novels into all my courses early in my teaching, but novels are just text. Poetry's elusive nature and its quagmire of allusions give me vertigo.

The next day, Hannah arrived with a copy of Adrienne Rich's *An Atlas of a Difficult World* (1991). Speaking out loud, she took me through a poem, once, twice, thrice, and more, each time showing me how the various words in different parts of the poem reflect, shadow, and echo each other in their connotations. As the page came alive for me, I could feel my body easing into the flow.

I still feel inadequately skilled to read poems without her presence. In fact, I think I finally understand the student anxiety that their college experience will abandon them as soon as they step off campus.

* * *

Students write stories about rape, incest, disease, suicide, and assault. They confess to relationships in which they are battered, and they admit to staying in violent situations. In one course, a third of my students recounted such stories. When I asked them to read each other's work, the course became more about these experiences than our putative subject matter.

Early on at Ithaca College, I wondered out loud with Sorayya if so much tragedy could really be a part of student life. Now I know. Students suffer all kinds of brutality. It's the "healthy" ones that require an explanation.

* * *

Theodor Adorno comes at teaching from a radically different perspective in his astonishing ten-page lecture, "Taboos of the Teaching Vocation."

Adorno wonders why society devalues teachers. While university professors, he suggests, receive more respect than their colleagues in schools, they, too, are painted with a degrading brush. Adorno responds to his question by speculating on society's "'unconscious' or 'preconscious' aversion to the teaching profession" (Adorno 1998 [1963], p. 178). He looks for taboos, which he defines as powerful "collective manifestation[s] of ideas . . . that have lost their real basis… and that nonetheless tenaciously persist as psychological and social prejudices and in turn influence reality" (p. 178).

Adorno then begins a series of speculations for which he admits he presents little evidence. He hopes that his exposition can produce hypotheses that lead to a research agenda.

He says that, historically, German society associates teachers with servants, monks, and scribes. Each of these derive ultimately from the role of slaves (p. 180). He further contends that since even today society is unified only by means of force, it is force and not ideas that carry the day (p. 183). Everyone, he insists, harbors the disdain that warriors carry for those who traffic in ideas instead of physical strength. He asserts that all of us, but especially children, strongly identify with the soldier (p. 180).

Society's contempt for teachers is due not merely to the bias that favors force, warriors, and soldiers. It is also that the pedagogue is a kind of non-expert; teachers, at least non-university teachers, usually have no specialization, and therefore, they are amateurs in all fields (p. 181).

Further, teachers' power is lowly since it merely commands children. Whereas judges and even administrators can lord it over adults, teachers' control of children infantilizes teachers (p. 181). We might say that teachers are child/adult hybrid entities who never attain the full status of adulthood (p. 184).

Teachers are also seen to be "unfair" and "not good sport[s]" (p. 182) because they necessarily have greater knowledge than the student, which they use to establish their authority and power. This rift is constitutive of the teacher-student relationship:

> Such unfairness—and every teacher, even the university teacher senses this—somewhat taints the advantage of the teacher's knowledge over that of his pupils, an advantage the teacher asserts without having the right, because indeed, the advantage is indivisible from his function, whereas he continually bestows upon that advantage an authority he can disregard only with great difficulty. (p. 182)

Adorno summarizes: "Unfairness lies . . . in the ontology of the teacher. . . ." (p. 182).

The difference between Parker Palmer and Theodor Adorno is that the latter thinks of society as essentially riven and then forcefully constituted as a unity. Thus, three elements define society: (1) essential divisions, whether they are on the axis of culture, politics, or economics, (2) the power used to contain and suture that division, and, most important, (3) the denial of the first two elements. Adorno describes this denial by saying, "It is essential for the inner structure of this complex that the physical violence any society based on domination requires must at all costs *not be acknowledged,* insofar as the society takes itself to be bourgeois-liberal" (p. 183, emphasis added).

Adorno derives two further claims from this statement. Force must not be acknowledged as the Real (to use Lacanian language) of the classroom, and the teacher is the entity who sustains the fiction that force is unnecessary—both in the classroom and in society. Society requires teachers to personify force in the classroom while also requiring teachers to deny the centrality of that force.

Adorno concludes that society can "achieve the so-called integration . . . only with the potential of physical violence" (p. 183). As such, the unconscious imagery of the teacher is as a "flogger" (p. 182), a "jailer," and a "drill sergeant" (p. 183). (The film *Whiplash* (2014), for example, certainly portrays the music teacher, Fletcher, as a drill sergeant breaking his students' wills.) Adorno writes,

> I consider this complex, even after the abolition of corporal punishment, to be decisive for the taboos on the teacher's vocation. This imago presents the teacher as the physically stronger who beats the weaker. . . . [t]his function [is] still ascribed to him even after the official function was abolished . . . (p. 182).

For Adorno, undoing this image of the teacher as a castigator requires going beyond the abolition of corporal punishment. What is further necessary is the disappearance of the "last memory trace of corporal punishment" in schools (p. 183).

If the historical traces and the macro-sociological context weren't enough, Adorno turns to problems of psychology. Children learn that "parents do not live up to the ego ideal they instill in their children" (p. 186). Children then encounter the teacher as a second opportunity with which to identify their ego ideal. But here too, they are let down because teachers are themselves former children who produced unsatisfying projections on to their own parents and their own teachers. Estranged societies cannot but produce both alienated students and alienated teachers (p. 186).

This complex of problems, which Adorno also calls an "archaism," is internalized by teachers, and it expresses itself as "bickering, grousing, scolding, and the like and in reactions that are always close to physical violence and betray a certain weakness and lack of self-confidence" (p. 187). Adorno endorses psychoanalytic training for teachers.

He closes the article by asking, "What is to be done?" Of course, the cure inheres in his diagnosis: the most important element is to create "enlightenment about the entire complex" (p. 188). This means producing a frank, honest, and clear-eyed assessment of the magnitude of the problem. In case we think that such a fix might be quick, Adorno warns that "one should not expect too much from intellectual engagement alone" and that we should "target the ideology of schooling" (p. 188).

He ends on what I experience as his most powerful insight: teaching and reforms to teaching should work within the process of "debarbarization." "By barbarism I do not mean the Beatles, although their cult is related to it, but the utmost extreme: delusional prejudice, oppression, genocide, and torture. . . ." (p. 190).

Delusion, oppression, genocide, and torture are what society, schooling, and teaching support. To substantiate this claim, Adorno brings the full weight of his historical experience of living through World War II and Nazi Germany:

> My generation experienced the relapse of humanity into barbarism in the literal, indescribable, and true sense. Barbarism is a condition where all the formative, cultivating influence, for which the school is responsible, *is shown to have failed.* It is certain that as long as society itself engenders barbarism, the school can offer only minimal resistance to it. But if barbarism, the horrible shadow over our existence, is, in fact, the contrary to culture, then it is also essential that individuals become debarbarized. (p. 190, emphasis mine)

Schooling, indeed the Enlightenment itself, has already failed. We are in the middle of a second try. As I once heard Sun Ra say during a concert, "It's after the end of the world, don't you know that yet?" Our first step then is to understand how schooling, society, and "civilization" align with barbarism.

* * *

Adorno's depth, sweep, and precision resonate. And yet somehow, he omits the thing that teachers protect most fervently, which is the prohibition against theorizing our teaching practice. It's not difficult to understand *why* we do this. As Thomas Rickert points out, we teachers, "tend to believe in the power of education. We risk much in doubting that power" (2007, 5). Our most fortified doubt is that teaching might do nothing to change the world; such disbelief leaves us with no claim on doing good or being good.[3] The adage, "Those who can, do. Those who cannot, teach" misses that, really, we are all teachers.

* * *

Tamar's speech was difficult for me to understand. I continuously asked her to repeat herself in class. Then I took to translating her words back to her and asking, "Is this what you mean?" I found her written work still more challenging. I had a category for such work: "Not even tenth-grade level." My assessment of her technical skills wasn't inaccurate, but I got everything else wrong.

In the first year of my teaching, I decided that I would not outsource those in my charge to the university's writing labs.[4] If a student did not have "even tenth grade" writing skills, I made it my job to get them to competence. This decision meant that I would work with the very ba-

---

3. ". . . pedagogies can function as a fantasy screen, allowing us to escape from the traumatic reality that our pedagogies do very little to change the actual injustices occurring throughout the world" (Rickert 2007, 107). And, "We insist upon seeing our minds as heroic witnesses to truth, when in fact they are characteristically paralyzed and disabled by ideals and beliefs that are emotionally uncomfortable" (Alcorn 2013, 21).

4. When I saw that students had inadequate writing skills, I wondered about my responsibility. Eventually, I decided it was mine. I told them I would not send them to the various writing tutors on campus. In part, this is because I've developed my ideas about writing. For me, writing is that process which transcribes internal emotion into external script. What is inside comes to be realized in the outer world. Recently, I have moved to a more Lacanian mode. I am trying to get students to strike a balance between control and its absence in their writing. Too much control allows for the execution of a predetermined plan, but the student does not learn anything *from* the writing process. Too little control means that the architecture is insufficiently developed to allow the ideas to inhabit the work. In both cases, I like to say that 'the writing will not write back.' When the balance is right, on the other hand, the writing does write back. This is the crucial moment. Striking that equilibrium between form and improvisation, between superego and the unconscious allows for surprises, moments where the writer marvels at the novelty of what emerges and embraces the role of becoming the writing's audience.

Getting the writing to write back is what I practice with my students. In reading their papers, I look for two elements. The elements of dominance and control and imperialism that they impose on their work is easy to gauge. But there's always something else. Something beyond their tacit control that speaks back to them. Something that they are not saying explicitly but formulating implicitly, despite their resistance. I look for the tension between the explicit and the implicit, for the space where this counter-theme seems to talk back. Then I ask the students how they account for the presence of these two elements? Once this project is underway it runs away with itself and there little left for me to do.

sics of writing. My techniques included all the following: Asking them for a one-paragraph version of their paper. Asking for a postproduction outline, showing them a process that I call a reverse outline, a sketch not of what they intended but what they actually produced on paper. Asking them to remove all jargon. Asking them to produce a tape recording of their ideas and then transcribe it. Writing a letter, perhaps to their best friend or to me. And most embarrassing for the students, asking them to read their papers out loud to me. For this last request, I might pull in another student from the waiting room so that the writer might see that even four ears cannot understand their work.

Even after all that, I wasn't guaranteed clean sentences or clear thoughts. Such failure had seismic repercussions for my pedagogy. In a pique of frustration, I would tell such students, "Write me anything you want." The students always had the same response, "Really? Anything?" "Yes, anything," I would say in exasperation. This, too, might not work if the student continued to believe that course themes had to be covered. I would say, "Please write me something that is important to you, something you really care about." Without fail, I would receive crisp, clean, clear prose. Without fail, such writing was always about one of two themes. It concerned some deep pain—a rape, a suicide, a confrontation with serious illness, a desire to die. Or it was about the student's anger at being forced to go to college.

As a result of that process, over a decade or so, I eventually come up with the prompt-less prompt, "Please write about something that is important to you." I tried this first in my upper-level courses and then, eventually, in all courses.

Tamar passed my first class because I could not deny her seriousness of purpose, her powerful presence in class, and her tangible curiosity. But I also took a risk by passing someone who could not write well.

Near the end of the semester, she came to my office and posed a series of questions about my life, about my reason for being in academia, and about what I hoped to accomplish in my teaching. I couldn't identify her motive. I was confused for twenty minutes before I recognized the form: she was interrogating me. If I was assessing her writing and speaking, she was assessing my very being. She concluded, "I think I could work with you," and with that, she let me know that I had passed her test.

As we worked on her writing, and as the semesters passed, I came to depend on her insight. I invited her to enroll in my honors class because I knew she would shake things up. We were reading *King Leopold's Ghost* (1999), in which Adam Hochschild counter-poses Belgian King Leopold's genocide of ten million Congolese with the heroic efforts of the Britisher E. D. Morel and the Irishman Roger Casement, whose journalism exposed Leopold's crime to the world. My purpose in using this book was to learn something about these events. I also hoped the students would see the historical relations between First and Third Worlds. Never mind that the heroes themselves were Westerners; at least they were revealing what to me were the most dangerous Western wrongs.

All of us except Tamar fell for Hochschild's neat binary. Over and over, she repeated with venom, "I hate Morel, I hate Morel."[5] It took me nearly ten minutes of working with her to fathom her response. Morel, she understood, was exposing Belgium but ignoring the same crimes perpetrated by the British. He was no good guy.

That sank me for a minute. How had I had missed it? My students, at least, had reasons to overlook it because they needed to believe that Westerners could do good. If even Morel should be hated for his duplicity, for his blindness to British crimes of the same magnitude as Leopold's, then what room did this leave for their own desire to remain untainted by the war crimes of the US government? All this thinking occurred subliminally, body to body.[6]

By the time she had fully elaborated her points, four students were openly crying, including the president of the Ithaca chapter of Amnesty International.[7] Who knew that a book could overturn your life and expose your career plans as a form of what Hochschild calls "evangelical imperialism?"[8]

---

5. "Thought is not simply linguistic representation of abstract ideation; thought extends in subtle ways into the emotional physiology of the body that can be read in the emotional gestures of the face" (Alcorn 2013, 67–8).

6. "Knowing can entail a loss of friends, loss of an imagined future, and a loss of established frames of emotional maturity" (Alcorn 2013, 128).

"Often, when we try to think about 'what is true,' we discover that 'what is true' is experienced as an act of violence attacking that which we love" (Alcorn 2013, 163).

7. "We insist upon seeing our minds as heroic witnesses to truth, when in fact they are characteristically paralyzed and disabled by ideals and beliefs that are emotionally uncomfortable" (Alcorn 2013, 21).

8. Hochschild, Adam. (1999). King Leopold's Ghost (New York: Houghton Mifflin), p. 212.

Tamar's precision and insistence forced me to reread the book and to develop her interpretation, the full version of which can be found in an article I wrote soon after.[9]

* * *

The course design of "Writing and Criticism" allows students to work for each other, and it does so despite the absence of incentives.

It meets twice a week for seventy-five minutes each. Tuesdays are "theory" days. We read Alcorn, Rickert, and others whose texts are difficult for me, and I introduce them by saying, "I don't expect you to understand these books. I am working through them, and you are welcome to join me." I was surprised when most of the students read, came prepared, and were eager to decode the material. This is the pattern in every iteration of the course.

Thursdays are "lab" days on which I ask for volunteers to make "offerings" to the class—essays, stories, poems, plays, films, anything they have created. Their offerings become our assignments. In class, everyone presents an appraisal/critique of the offered work. I present my critique of each student's critique. The author of the work is asked not to speak until the following week when they are given five minutes to respond.

At first, students offer their essays written for other classes. If their essay had been graded poorly, they might see how it fares in our class. Or, more typically, they are suspicious of their own well-graded work and wish to offer it for our criticism. Soon, however, as the bonds form, they start writing for our community. These offerings can be short, or they can be twenty pages. In one case, we went to a performance of a student's play.

Initially, I did not know if students would take me up on the offerings. They hesitate at first, but typically by mid-semester, the schedule for the final seven weeks is full. Almost everyone wishes to participate. Here, too, the course offers no grading incentive to make offerings, but they appear anyway.

Their grade is based on five five-page written critiques during the semester. Here is the description from the syllabus:

---

9. *International Studies Perspectives* (2012) under the title, "The Dark Heart of Kindness."

My primary evaluative method will be to criticize your written work, namely the five critiques that constitute most of your grade. I plan to assess and comment on your written criticism. Your critiques can incorporate the writing of professionals, if you like. They can aim at your own prior work. You can comment on the written work of your colleagues in the class—should they volunteer their work for public comment. You can criticize film, music, drama, literature, a meal at a restaurant, or another's' criticism. Or you can offer your own criticism of any aspect of popular culture.

Along with a final comprehensive paper, the critiques account for their grade. One reason I love the course is that it is exhilarating to see how seriously they take each other's work. Their work gives me something I seem to need, namely, the vitality that emerges from internalizing criticism as faith.

* * *

The film *Waterland* (1992) follows a high school history teacher, Tom Crick, who supplements traditional methods with risqué stories of his teenage life, including scenes depicting his own sexuality and his confrontation with abortion, incest, murder, and betrayal. His students are alternatively mesmerized by his story-telling risks and repulsed by his disclosure of intimacies. They, along with the film's audience, wonder how soon it will be before Crick is busted by parents or the school administration.

His students often intervene in his narratives by questioning his methods. Specifically, they want to know why he tells stories. As a master of timing, he lingers on the question, turning it back to them, "What do you think I am doing?"

Judy, an eager student who exhibits clear signs of transference, answers earnestly: "You want to show that you were a part of the history we are learning, just as we are. . . ."[10]

The suspicious and aggravated Matthew Price thinks Judy is obsequious. Crick senses the opportunity and asks Price to articulate his own interpretation:

---

10. Quotes are paraphrases in this segment unless otherwise depicted with indentations.

Price: "I think you are trying to buy us off. I think you are scared that no one is listening to your lousy history lessons anymore so you are starting to make things up, stories about schoolgirls fucking, just to keep us quiet, so that you can get in with us, but you can't because you are just a teacher."

Crick ponders Price's response but is unhurried. Price, however, cannot wait and reverts to his role as student:

Price: "Am I right? I am right."

Crick: "Might be. So might you be, Judy."

In the film, we can note Crick's use of delay, non-certainty, and deflection. More important is Price's insinuation that the teacher's motive is to "get in" with the students, a vain ploy because Crick is *"just a teacher"*—a lowly figure, as Adorno explained. The teacher is not a part of history but just its reporter, not part of the student community but just a has-been with no chance of changing the world. Price exposes the central fissure between teacher and students and stresses Crick's futility.

Still, there is another way to consider Crick's performance. Consider the following quote from Henry Kariel's "Becoming Political":

> [Good political actors/artists] include parts of themselves in their field of operation, communicating both what they do and what transpires in their minds. They show themselves opening up, taking things in, changing in the process of observing. In each instance, as they exhibit themselves, they become the spokesmen of uninhibited elements in the lives of others. They represent suppressed realms of being. (Kariel 1977, 140)

Crick is showing himself, changing himself as he tells his story, and this allows Judy to uncover repressed elements of her own life. No wonder she is engrossed and engaged. Price, on the other hand, seems to be saying, "I am on to you, you want to deny the difference between us. You might seduce Judy with your embarrassing stories, but I am here to call your bluff."

Kariel continues: "And just as their acts threaten to become unbearable—just before we shudder and break out in embarrassed laughter or tears—they enable us to *see*" (p. 140, emphasis original). Crick has already become unbearable for Price, causing him to shudder in embarrassment. Why, we might wonder, is Crick willing to risk such an evaluation, such rejection?

Later in the film, Crick and Price meet at a pub:

Crick: "You weren't very fond of my stories…"

Price: "…Not at first. But I thought you were telling them for us…I thought, 'Hey, give me a break.' Then I thought you were doing it for yourself, and I thought that's okay. . . . I didn't mind that."

Crick: "Strange, I thought I was telling them for you. . . . I thought you were scared. That's what you do for children when they're scared, you tell them stories."

Price mistrusts Crick until he discerns that his stories emerged from Crick's effort to heal himself. Orthogonally, Crick thinks his stories bypass and encircle students' fear of reality, of the actual events within which they live. While we might say, parroting Crick's response earlier above, "It might be that both Price and Crick are correct," we might nevertheless note the divide between their interpretations. The film builds its narrative *on* that fault line, *in* that fissure.

* * *

One day, a friend who teaches elsewhere shared a confidence: his colleague was miserable because a student's suicide note mentioned the colleague's name.

My instant thought was that I could not continue as a teacher if that ever happened to me. Looking back at my career, at my risk-prone, psychologically saturated teaching methods, and at the intimacy that very often develops with students, I have to count myself as fortunate (knock on wood, please).

This does not mean there haven't been close calls. There have. After graduation, two of my students informed me about their unsuccessful attempts. Again, my reaction was anger. It goes something like this: "You seem to think your life is yours to end. Have you no concern for others? Why didn't you see that your attempt would devastate us—your friends, your parents, and your teachers? Who do you think you are? God?"

I know this candor makes me a nonviable candidate for the suicide prevention hotline.

I had an even stronger reaction when one of my first students, Professor Will Moore, ended his life. I feel unbearable loss and mourning that I can barely describe but also anger at the severing of the community.

When Chris Smith, who likes to go by the moniker "Master of the Universe," visited me after his unsuccessful suicide attempt, he made me rethink my position.

He conveyed that he felt he was going on only for other people's sake, implying an absence of an inner desire to live. I let him know that I did not want to be a part of his burden, that he needn't live simply to satisfy my desire for his company. I said, "Maybe my attitude just places you under more pressure. Feel free to do what you need."

I know the best counter to my initial attitude: the present is perfect. Meaning: the contemplated, attempted, or successful suicide is already the best solution to an impossible situation. What I need to address is not the agent's willfulness but the structure that creates the impossible situation. Social theory, to say nothing of wisdom, is no more than this.

We are back to that extraordinary question produced by Paulinho Chamon and Eddie Dowd in class that day: "Do you, or don't you, feel as if you have to justify your existence on this planet?" I can see across this essential fissure to the other side, but my stride is not long enough nor my heart calm enough to set foot there,[11] but perhaps a few more conversations with Chris can quell my ire and point me to the path of understanding.

* * *

Phillip wrote a fifteen-page paper for his first assignment. Long papers are not usually an issue for me. I ask for between five to eight pages but will read on if the writing engages me. Phillip's did not. Indeed, I stopped reading after three pages and called him into my office.

I have only recently learned that writers are hurt by the abrupt ending to the reading responsibility. I was reading a paper co-authored by two of my favorite colleagues, but I could not make sense of its prose, organization, or purpose. Five pages in, I wrote on the margins: "I stopped reading here." The message is simple: "After a good faith effort, I could not get beyond this page. I could skim the rest while pretending to have read it, but I think it might be useful for you to know exactly where I stopped reading."

---

11. Laura McNeal responds: "Those who feel the need to justify often fail, and when they fail too often, they think they shouldn't be here. It seems like arrogance, but I think it's a failure to be arrogant enough." Laura's diagnosis forces me to replace my anger with a different medicine, for which I don't quite have the words yet.

I make this move often with students. I want them to understand what my colleagues already know, which is that my reading of their work is not part of my work obligation. If the writing does not engage me even as I make a full effort, I stop.

Phillip came to my office and shouted at me. I can still see the fury on his face so close to violence. He forced himself to calm down and to convey to me the fantastic effort he had made, the greatness of his work that I would discover if only I read on, and how deeply my disrespect hurt him.

I explained that I considered myself a responsible pedagogue. I elucidated firmly that, in fact, it was my job *not* to read his work past the point of my interest and beyond my ability to focus on it. If I can assess the paper's poor quality in the first few pages, I can skim the rest. I asked him to rewrite the paper but this time in three pages.

The following week, he gave me another fifteen-page paper, again incomprehensible, and again, I put it down after three pages. When I returned it, he read my comments and, in a flurry, left class. I did not fail to notice the hard looks he threw my way. After class, in the hallway, he confronted me. His vehemence made me glad to be in a public space and between classes.

I had several thoughts on the walk back to my office. I wondered where I had parked my car and whether Phillip knew what I drove, I wondered if he knew my home address, and I wondered how I might protect my family.

I have failed to mention that outside of these encounters over his writing, Phillip was dedicated to my methods and to me. He had what I took to be a sincere desire to engage in conversation and to talk about how the ideas in our work together were changing his life. If we can speak in such terms, I would say that there was love there. But that love alchemized, as an admiring love sometimes does, into hatred.

After we somehow survived the course together, I still feared enough for my safety to ask Phillip never to contact me again. I count that experience as a failure, of course. And I don't know how I might have moved us to a successful relationship.

* * *

Laura Oriol sat in my office, looking at Lake Cayuga, as she re-counted how her parents, in separate conversations with her, shared their childhood traumas, their pains, and their defeats. They used her ears, she told to me in visit after visit, as sounding boards, placing her in the role of a therapist. They reversed the parent-child relationship.

Finally, I intervened: "What they are doing to you is wrong. You need to stand up for your rights as a child. They gave birth to you, not you to them. They have to account to your needs, not you to theirs."

Sometimes, I take the risk before I have fully calculated. Lights went on for both of us. I reviewed my family life from the lens of my assertions.

* * *

At the Pittsburgh airport, Stefan Senders, now a bread maker and owner of Wide Awake Bakery, but at the time a graduate student, ap-proached me and went straight to his point. "I read your chapter in the Lapid and Kratochwil book," he said. "You are so close but also so wrong. You think we travel to know, but we travel to heal."

My response was instant: "What are you reading that allows you this insight?" He gave me a list, mostly of Slavoj Zizek's books, and I became Stefan's student.

CHAPTER 8

Epilogue

Projection, Transference, Embodiment

My former student Kim Correll was visiting Ithaca from Brooklyn. At dinner, she said, "I'm forty, which means I am about the age you were when I first took your class." She was there to tell me of my large influence in her life. "I wanted to tell you now and not at your funeral." I am, of course, deeply moved by her words, but I am also confused. Her gift seems disproportionate to my effort. Much of our dinner was my trying to locate the source of her good will.

Sue Lambe was visiting Ithaca from Massachusetts. In our first few minutes together, she said, "I am forty now. An adult. Which means I am the age you were when we first met." She shared her gratitude for my influence on her effusively.

She didn't allow me my usual structural deflections whereby I suggest that students only project their love onto the object that happens to be my body, and that I had done the same with my teachers. Sue is a clinical psychologist, and all day long, she works with projection, counter-projection, transference, and countertransference. "I know all about projection," she said, "but there is some part of this process that is unique, singular, that is only about you. Isn't there?"

Again, I invited her to think with me about how that "magic" happens. She indulged me as we worked on this question. But this was my project, not hers. She drove to Ithaca, in part, to feel the delight of expressing her gratitude. She's accomplished her mission, but mine continues.

Consider what Lacan says about transference: "As soon as there is somewhere a subject presumed to know, there is transference." And,

"Transference is love. . . . I insist: it is love directed toward, addressed to, knowledge."[1] Here, Lacan reveals the misdirection, the displacement I mumbled to Kim and to Sue. Love, love of knowledge, cannot stick to an abstraction; it adheres to bodies. Tangible unique persons become talismans. As Lacan insists, love is always love of knowledge, but to manifest, it must travel towards someone. Love, love of knowledge, is a species of travel.[2]

My friend and co-conspirer Paulinho Chamon wrote something similar. I claimed in a previous paper ("Teaching is Impossible") that while I was busy trying to get my students to understand the structured nature of global inequality, they instead "simply wanted to express their joy at being in my classroom." Naren Kumarakulasingam highlighted this passage because he found the claim extraordinary. Naren's observation caught Paulinho's ear and led to Paulinho's analysis:[3]

> I have been struggling to understand this joy since Naren pointed it out. Here is my latest thought: *this, too, is projection.* They project that you are a source of their enjoyment. You are not. But they place you in that position. They are working through their own possibilities of enjoyment. That is the secret, yes?

I am captivated by Paulinho's analysis, but I suspect that Kim and Sue would still point out that there must be a reason why their love

1. Quoted in Felman, S. (1982). "Psychoanalysis and Education," *Yale French Studies*, 63: p. 35.
2. Hannah Gignoux responds: "It can be both, God damn it. But when it comes to the 'influence' you've had on our lives, I see where the diagnosis might be appropriate. One day during Summer Scholars, you wrote something on a set of notes I had sent you in which you called my work brilliant or something like this. Every paper you'd return to me with praise and I would break down in tears. Tears because I could not accept my own skills and motivation and love of learning. It felt like a responsibility. Rather than accept this responsibility it is easier to deflect or project the impact of my own work onto you, the mentor. I know this is a false move, and yet it lightens the weight of my own investment in learning.
At the same time, love for you can exist in the same way in which I love my peers and family that have been around to shape me. It's a community. I think that the reason that I react so strongly to your resistance to Kim and Sue is because I hear you as saying that their love is misplaced and projected. But now I am realizing that you are saying that it is their insistence on your influence that is misplaced. They want to confess their gratitude toward the method and theory that you deploy, but this is too abstract, and so they turn to you."
3. Personal correspondence. Paulinho continues: "Our work, then, is to disallow the liberal affective framework to capture their joy [and convert it] into a cycle of consumption. The potential for this escape [from the boredom of their partying] . . . is already there; if it wasn't, they would not need to work through that joy, they would not need to project it on to you, they would not need to wrap that projection as an expression of joy."

of knowledge directs itself to my body. Even as I insist, in turn, that all I am trying to do is heal myself in their presence and with their assistance. They see the unique structure of the snowflake. I point to the anonymous dust at its center.

* * *

Sue reads the previous vignette, and it drives her to anger and then to sadness. There is something I am not understanding and something that she is trying to express to me in our last dozen exchanges. She has located the characteristic that she believes she has internalized from watching me as "authority *without* domination," a non-domination that is related to my willingness to learn from students, she says. It is to express this to me, finally, that she drives to Ithaca.

* * *

There are some students that I never again want to meet. I can count a dozen immediately. Their names and my encounters with them still fill me variously with rage, shame, defeat, and a lingering sense that I remain inadequate in my patience, my diagnostic skills, my compassion, my empathy, and my work ethic. They will never see me if I see them first, on campus, in Ithaca, or anywhere at all.

* * *

For decades in class, I have regularly doled out "bonus points" to students when I appreciate their contribution. When, finally, a student asks, "What are these bonus points worth?" I pause an extra two beats before delivering the answer: "Bonus points are worth a lot. With them and $1.35 you can get a small coffee, don't you know."

In my Rio class one day, Paulinho Chamon responded to one of my comments with this: "Good one professor. Bonus points." I cannot recall what I said to merit his praise, but it was the first and only time I had received "bonus points" from a student. Since then, I have been working to receive more points from Paulinho. Academics don't really need material incentives, just opportunities for bonus points, a non-secret exploited by every administrator.

* * *

I know what to do when students express hostility, defiance, and anger; their expressed feelings become resources for the classroom. However, I have not solved what to do with passive-aggression. I've learned to search for passive-aggressive students, but even when I find them, what do I do? Please send suggestions.

* * *

Sophia Morris went well beyond what I asked of the class. Recalling my days with Bruce Longden in ninth-grade geography class at the Lyceé des Nations in Geneva, it occurred to me that I still remember economic and political details about Trinidad and Tobago, Senegal, and Gambia. I remember them only because Mr. Longden asked us to produce maps of those places. I did so happily with tracing paper and colored pencils.

On a whim, I asked each student in my honors course on "Afghanistan and Origins of Global Fury" to draw a map of Afghanistan. Most found my request infantilizing. Sophia, on the other hand, dedicated hours to it. Its beauty and care are still on display just outside my office.

Sophia was also an employee of our department. While she was delivering the mail one day, we fell into a more in-depth conversation than usual. She told me how one night her father had given her advice. It is crucial, he said, to "make the ask." Before you go to bed, ask for what you need—from God or the Cosmos or whatever entity you harbor as divine.

Since then, I rarely go to bed without making "the ask." I put my subconscious to work, and often, I wake up with a gift.

* * *

The applause I received from students at the beginning of my career has not returned. Praise has taken on other forms.

I am on the third floor of Williams Hall in one of my favorite classroom spaces. It is nearly the end of the semester, and the students seem relaxed, satisfied that they had gained something. One of them near the west window cannot contain himself, "You've really made this into a great class." Ever eager to deflect, I respond, "We did this together, right?" Now many more of them chime in, all in harmony, "Well, really, it was you."

For years, I have heard talk from students about the "cult"—a group that takes all my courses, hangs out mainly with each other, and disdainfully excludes others, as if they command some secret. Other students complain that they didn't take my course because they were put-off by the behavior of "my cult."[4]

Worried, I started pointing to my method. Once a session, I explained some part of my actions—why I ask my four questions at the start, the reasons for the geometry of the classroom, my use of silences, why I stop calling on overeager talkers, why we read passages aloud. I end with the mantra, "It's a method. Anyone can replicate it."

That didn't work. It merely deepened their resolve to tag my body. They said, "Sure, it's a method, but you are the one who developed it." As my former chair once said to me, by way of dismissal, "Only you can do this."[5]

Replicability is important to me. I understand that science is a kind of faith—we assume that the universe is ordered, that we can know that order, and that we can change it. But science has one or two advantages over the institution we call "religion." Replicability is the most important of these.

Denise Nuttall, a Canadian with a love of Indian music, is one of my favorite colleagues. She has mastered the tabla by training with the great *Ustad* Zakir Hussain. Her published work describes how her *Ustad* appears in her dreams to continue the lesson and how she learned that all *Ustad* Zakir's students share this experience. I am astonished by Denise's devotion to Indian music and her commitment to the mentor-disciple (Guru-Shishya) relationship. She and her methods are a force of nature.

---

4. Emma Kast responds: "I had indeed heard a few students . . . say they didn't take a class with you because they were put off by the 'cult.' But I also heard others say they knew they would have probably benefited from the course but didn't want to have their entire worlds fall apart, thank you very much."

5. David Blaney responds: "I suspect that this is true. Maybe some elements are replicable, but this is not just another technique or best practice that can be taken off the shelf and implemented as a module in a classroom. This 'method' is interwoven with your person. It's why what I do overlaps with what you do in the classroom, but why it is also quite different at some points, since my classroom work is also interwoven with my person and that sets some limits on what I can do unless I change or am changed. I do know I learned some things from coming to your classroom (and again from reading this) that I wonder if I can find them in myself so that I can make them part of my classroom."

When team teaching together, I am mesmerized by her desire to bring the Guru-Shishya[6] form to our campus, which is a form I find myself rejecting.

Late in his life, my father set out to repair the yawning rift between us by taking me on a tour of villages in the Punjab. That job had been my mother's because my father, alienated from his origins, had refused it. When his kin came to visit us in the city, they invariably returned to the village disappointed and furious that my father had done nothing to procure them employment there. He could not return to his village without his stay turning into a days-long defense of his decisions. It was not possible for him to bridge his belief in meritocracy with his relatives' conviction that his standing in the city belonged to the village as a whole. With that deadlock, it became my mother's responsibility to transport us from the glass heights of cosmopolitan cities to the grounding depths of adobe villages.

In his retirement, however, my father reclaimed his role as guide to his children. Our first stop was my mother's village, Kolo-Tarar, to pay respects to my Nani, my mother's mother and the only grandparent my siblings and I knew. There, I saw my father perform a scene that, while not atypical for Pakistanis, was nevertheless impossible for me to imagine given his assimilation into modern Western life. He made himself supine to touch my Nani's feet with his head. As he bent down, she placed her hand under his chin, lifted his head with her hands, disallowing a completion of the gesture, and thereby playing her part in this drama. This, he was showing me, is how one treats elders (and teachers).

I am sure that Denise would not hesitate to submit to Zakir Hussain in this way. In contrast, I do not imagine anyone to whom I would offer my kinesthetic obeisance. Not because I am not awed by greatness, but because I worry about this ideal. I aim neither to lead nor to follow but to walk side by side.[7] In this way, Denise is more South Asian than I am.

---

6. Loosely translated as a mentoring relationship in which the master transmits learning to the disciple.

7. Emma Kast: "But you also believe distance creates intimacy. Side by side, yes, but with distance, could we say?"

My commitment to replicability goes hand in hand, in a manner of speaking, with a rejection of the Guru-Shishya model, cult of personality, and personal praise.

I eventually realized that highlighting my teaching method would simply go unnoticed by most of my students. They would continue attributing their experience to me and ignore the method. My continued failure led me to develop the course titled "Writing and Criticism." Ostensibly, it's designed to demonstrate how to write and how to criticize. But its deeper purpose is to probe the question, *Are learning and teaching at all possible?*

The course became imaginable only when Sara-Maria Sorentino responded to my confession that I was no longer able to read Paulo Freire's work because it relied too much on the possibility of "liberation."[8] She recommended books by Marshall Alcorn and Thomas Rickert.

I devoured their texts with the thirst and craving of someone who had finally stumbled into an oasis. Alcorn's and Rickert's Zizekian foundation assume an unbridgeable fissure in the classroom between teacher and student, the impossibility of teaching, and the unlikeliness of learning due to the stickiness of psychological, sociological, and historical structures. In their writing, I recognized the implicit teleology of my own career.[9] More encouragingly, they highlight the skills one can develop if one submits to teaching's impossibility.

If the "Writing and Criticism" course did not dissolve my "cult of personality" problem, I reasoned, nothing would. I have offered the course eight times, but I don't think this problem will go away. The writing you are reading is, in part, my continuing effort to sort out the structural from the idiosyncratic. If only I, alone, can perform this pedagogy, then it dies with me.

* * *

A rare compliment I can absorb came from Alicia Williams. She sat in my office gazing out at Cayuga Lake, her muscle tension and posture expressing urgency. Nevertheless, she stayed quiet for a good

---

8. As does bell hooks in *Teaching to Transgress*, Routledge 1994.

9. "A postpedagogy, insofar as it declines to participate in the dialectics of control, is an exhortation to dare, to invent, to create, to risk. It is less a body of rules, a set of codifiable classroom strategies, than a willingness to give recognition to unorthodox, unexpected, or troublesome work" (Rickert 2007, 196).

three minutes. It was our second class together, and she was assessing my role in our experience. "You do your job," she finally says. Yes, yes, yes.

Shaun Poust produces a similar assessment, albeit, with tongue firmly in cheek. He says, "Your pedagogy is a lightning rod, and our society is a prairie in a thunderstorm." He continues:

> I insist, [good] as you and your method are, it is because they are com-
> pared with what is basically glorified professional training and policing
> that they look not only excellent, but miraculous. We are in a desert, and
> you happen to have some water. Hell, I'll give you a little bit of credit:
> you have water and margaritas and a pool table. But we *are* in a desert.

Here is Shaun's nutshell description of what I do:

> You . . . listen to a bunch of people and then ask them questions. That's
> what you get. That's also what you get if you're a student in one of your
> classes; it takes a while for people to notice that. . . . your entire teaching
> career amounts to—but is so much more than—an immense and compli-
> cated quantitative and qualitative survey.

Water, margaritas, a pool table, and questions.

* * *

One writes to say something but also to read what one writes. I am surprised by three messages this writing sends me.[10]

I now sympathize with my colleagues and my administrators. I put them in difficult and impossible situations. *How*, I wonder, *did they put up with my adventures?*[11] Well, mostly, they didn't, but I am amazed with their willingness to tolerate me. It was tolerance, not acceptance,

---

10. Sam Boyles comments: "The last section . . . makes me wonder if there is a desire to call something forth in the act of brinksmanship. The surprise at others' willingness to tolerate the narrator is . . . telling. I experience a similar emotion daily in my classes and work. I wonder if it is something about expressing something we are pretty sure people do not want to hear and hoping they will still be with us—like there is a boundary testing going on in some way, shape, or form."

11. My risk proneness in pedagogy is risk aversion in other domains. For example, I have refused all offers to talk about or teach on the Middle East, I stayed away from public discussions on 9/11/2001, and I only recently admitted that my training in a Hegelian critique of Marx still leaves me in the Marxian tradition. I only need consider the public (and official) treatment of figures such as Paul Robeson, Ward Churchill, and Susan Sontag to trigger my self-censorship. Perhaps we are all assorted combinations of risk attraction and risk repulsion.

intrigue, or cultivation.[12] Still, I'll admit I've been fortunate. In every position I held, I created the conditions that led to a precipice. How my family survived my brinkmanship, I don't know.

Anything might happen if we treat pedagogy as encounter. Anything.

Is this why so few of us take pedagogical risks and why teaching remains so undertheorized? If we do not police, if we do not securitize the classroom with the military geometry of rows and columns, if we do not benumb them with our lectures, if we do not threaten them with grades and attendance policies, *anything might happen*. The full plethora of human emotion might emerge, forcing us to practice at being a human being without a license. I understand better the risks of pedagogical encounters after writing this book. Thread by thread, encounters can undo our professionalism, until we stand naked and with nothing to say—as in our anxiety dreams.

That common dream is really a premonition and a challenge, no? Because fear is desire.

---

12. There are exceptions, and they include Sue Wadley, John Agnew, Margaret Himley, Denise Nuttall, Ron Denson, Katharine Kittridge, Catherine Taylor, Jason Freitag, and Leslie Lewis, the lone administrator in this group.

Afterword

I could tell the story of the origins of this book by turning to a late-night session in 2013 with students and colleagues at Vassar College, where Himadeep Muppidi teaches. Himadeep had the habit of inviting me to various events at his college, just a four-hour drive from Ithaca. That night, the conversation turned to teaching and the principles of pedagogy, not what worked and what didn't in the classroom. Rather, we (about a dozen students and a few colleagues) discussed what it meant to teach. Akta Kaushal took meticulous notes that she retrieved for me years later when I became serious about writing this book.

Or I could start with my sense that evening that I was reaching the end of my career. What a pity it would be, I lamented, if the practices and principles I had developed over a thirty-year career would vanish. Without knowing it, I was pulled to create and entrust an inheritance —itself built on what I'd received from my teachers. Paulinho Chamon reminds me that the transfer was already in process since many of my former students were practicing these methods and making them their own. I came to know this only after receiving comments on multiple drafts of this manuscript.

Or I could start the story with two sabbaticals. The first one led me to reread Paulo Freire. I was astonished at my disappointment. How could the torchbearer for all things pedagogical no longer inspire me? I realized I did not believe that teaching could move us towards liberation. I wasn't even sure that teaching was possible. And yet the classroom was still alive with possibility.

My plan for my more recent sabbatical was to take notes for a planned book with David Blaney on Marx and theories of exploitation. And, to write what I came to call the "pedagogy book," which I had been thinking about for years. From May to February, I took copious notes on Marx when Sorayya finally became concerned that I had not yet begun the pedagogy book. "If I start that book, it will take over my life," I said in defense. One day, in August 2019, just weeks before the start of classes, I started. Three weeks later, I had a draft. After two more weeks of editing, I thought I was done.

I sent the manuscript to dozens of friends, colleagues, and former students, expecting that only a few would read it and fewer would provide comments. To my surprise, most responded with plenty to say.

I received detailed comments from several people which pushed me to reshape the work: Laura McNeal, Elizabeth Dauphinee, Cory Brown, Sorayya Khan, Lori Amy, Paulinho Chamon, Hannah Gignoux, Sue Lambe, and Laura Oriol. Many commented on multiple versions of the manuscript. I completed a third draft and sent it out for review.

In June 2020, my friend, Joel Dinerstein, intervened. He said he appreciated the wave-like flow of my 120 autobiographical vignettes, but nevertheless, he was rearranging them into eight chapters. "I love the book you have, but the reader needs a little help with the organization," he said. I wasn't amenable to his suggestion. I was invested in the free-form nature of my arrangement in which the method of presentation followed the method of discovery. Joel anticipated my reluctance to consider what I came to call the "Joel re-mix." He sent the re-mix to Sorayya, who agreed that the new form improved the book. Outnumbered and outwitted, I overcame my reluctance and arranged the fourth draft.

A community is responsible for this work. My deep gratitude goes out to: Betsy Aleshire, Lori Amy, Richa and Medha Nagar, Kaela Bamberger, Ilan Baron, Shampa Biswas, David Blaney, Sam Boyles, Robert Brem, Cory Brown, Paulinho Chamon, Jeane Copenhaver-Johnson, Elizabeth Dauphinee, Joel Dinerstein, Jenny Edkins, Dean Freeman, Jamie Frueh, Hannah Gignoux, Carla Golden, Evgenia Ilieva, Frankey Ithaka, Emma Kast, Akta Kaushal, Naren Kumarakulasingham, Sue Lambe, Lori Leonard, Alex Lima, Taylor Long, Wayne Malcolm, Elliot Lowe, Laura McNeal, Laura Oriol, Andy Paras, Shaun Poust,

Brooke Reynolds, Manu Samnotra, Kate Schick, James Searl, Chris Smith, Patrick T. Jackson, Catherine Taylor, Chris Tolve, Andrew Voorhees, Huilan Xu, and eight anonymous reviewers. Jane Banks's astute editing and commentary was the final step. A special thanks to Sorayya Khan, who read all versions of this manuscript, has stood beside me through this pedagogical journey, and who has embraced its highs and lows.

The stories in this book reflect the author's recollection of events. Some names, locations, and identifying characteristics have been changed to protect the privacy of those depicted. Dialogue has been re-created from memory.

I dedicate this book to all those who engaged me in the contact zone of encounter. I thank you for meeting me there. You know who you are.

Ithaca
October 2021

Works Cited

Adorno, Theodor. (1998 [1963]). "Taboos of the Teaching Vocation," in *Critical Models: Interventions and Catchwords*. New York: Columbia University Press.

Alcorn, Marshall. (2002). *Changing the Subject in English Class: Discourse and the Constructions of Desire*. Carbondale, IL: Southern Illinois University Press.

Alcorn, Marshall. (2013). *Resistance to Learning: Overcoming the Desire Not to Know in Classroom Teaching*. New York: Palgrave Macmillan.

Brennan, Timothy. (2008). *Secular Devotion: Afro-Latin Music and Imperial Jazz*. New York: Verso.

Bull, Hedley. (1977). *The Anarchical Society*. New York: Columbia University Press.

Bull, Hedley, and Adam Watson. (1984). *The Expansion of International Society*. Oxford: Oxford University Press.

Collingwood, R. G. (1962). *The Idea of History*. Oxford: Clarendon Press.

Dickey, Laurence. (1987). *Hegel: Religion, Economics, and the Politics of Spirit, 1770–1807*. Cambridge: Cambridge University Press.

Du Bois, W. E. B. (1999 [1920]). "The Hands of Ethiopia," in *Darkwater: Voices from Within the Veil*. New York: Dover.

Felman, Shoshana. (1982). "Psychoanalysis and Education," *Yale French Studies,* 63:21–44.

Freire, Paulo. (1970). *Pedagogy of the Oppressed*. New York: Continuum.

hooks, bell. (1994). *Teaching to Transgress*. New York: Routledge.

Hochschild, Adam. (1999). *King Leopold's Ghost*. New York: Houghton Mifflin.

Griffin, Susan. (1998). "Happiness," in *Bending Home*. Port Townsend, WA: Copper Canyon Press

Inayatullah, Naeem, and David Blaney. (2012). "The Dark Heart of Kind-ness." *International Studies Perspectives* 13, (2):164–75.

Inayatullah, Naeem. (2019). "Why Do Some People Think They Know What Is Good for Others?" in Jenny Edkins and Maja Zehfuss (eds.), *Global Politics: A New Introduction, 3rd Edition.* New York: Routledge, pp. 430–53.

Inayatullah, Naeem. (2019). "Teaching is Impossible," in Jamie Frueh (eds.) *Pedagogical Journeys Through World Politics.* New York: Palgrave Macmillan.

Issak, Tamara. (2013). "The Politics of Pedagogy," interview by Tamara Issak for *This Rhetorical Life,* November 15, 2013. http://thisrhetoricallife.syr.edu/episode-15-the-politics-of-pedagogy-with-naeem-inayatullah/

Kariel, Henry. (1977). "Becoming Political," in Vernon van Dyke (eds.), *Teaching Political Science.* London: Humanities Press, pp. 129–45.

Laymon, Kiese. (2013). *How to Slowly Kill Yourself and Others in America.* Evanston, IL: Agate.

Lindqvist, Sven. (1977). *Exterminate the Brutes.* New York: New Press.

Mansbach, Richard, Yale Ferguson, and Donald Lampert. (1976). *The Web of World Politics: Non-State Actors in the Global System.* Hoboken, NJ: Prentice-Hall.

Maren, Michael. (2002). *The Road to Hell: The Ravaging Effects of Foreign Aid and International Charity.* New York: Free Press.

Marx, Karl. (1976). "Introduction to A Contribution to the Critique of Hegel's Philosophy of Right." In *Collected Works,* vol. 3. New York: International Publishers.

Nandy, Ashis. (1983). *The Intimate Enemy.* Oxford: Oxford University Press.

Palmer, Parker. (1993). *To Know as We Are Known: Education as a Spiritual Journey.* New York: Harper Collins.

Palmer, Parker. (1997). *The Courage to Teach.* Hoboken, NJ: Wiley.

Rickert, Thomas. (2007). *Acts of Enjoyment.* Pittsburgh, PA: University of Pittsburgh Press.

Said, Edward. (1979). *Orientalism.* New York: Vintage.

Shor, Ira and Paulo Freire. (1986). *Pedagogy for Liberation.* Westport, CT: Praeger.

Stavrianos, L. S. (1981). *Global Rift: The Third World Comes of Age.* New York: William Morrow.

Todorov, Tzvetan. (1999). *The Conquest of America.* Norman, OK: University of Oklahoma Press.

Veal, Michael. (2000). *Fela.* Philadelphia: Temple University Press.

Waterland. (1987). Stephen Gyllenhaal (director). New Line Cinema.

Whiplash. (2014). Damien Chazelle (director). Sony Pictures.

Wilson, Olly. (1983). "Black Music as an Art Form," *Black Music Research Journal* 3, pp. 1–22.

Weinrobe, Phil and Naeem Inayatullah. (2005). "A Medium of Others," in (ed) M. I. Franklin (ed.), *Resounding International Relations: On Music, Culture and Politics*, chapter 9. New York: Palgrave Macmillan.

Index

academics: inquisitor for, 25; professionalism of, 24n2, 127; role of, 30. *See also* teachers

Academy for Rural Development, 9–10

Achebe, Chinua, 29

Adorno, Theodor, 104–7

Afghanistan and the Origins of Global Fury course, 66, 78–79, 122

Alcorn, Marshall, 64, 125

aleatory processes, 48

Aleshire, Betsy, 68

Alex (student), 82

alienation, in society, 106

ambush, 36, 80

Andrew (student), 91–92

Andrew Neiman (fictional character), 94

announcements, 50

archive, 23

"the ask," 122

Assistant Dean, 37

Associate Dean, 47, 79

An Atlas of a Difficult World (Rich), 104

attendance, 45

authoritarian pedagogy, 43n12

Badaber Air Base, 9, 10

Baker, John, 34, 35, 36, 37–38

Bamberger, Kaela, 43n13

Bangash, Amaan Ali, 87

Bangash, Ayaan Ali, 87

barbarism, 107

Beachler, Don, 72

"Becoming Political" (Kariel), 30, 40, 113

Belia, Sal, 89–90

Blaney, David, 123n5, 130

body language, 47

"bonus points," 121

Boyles, Sam, 126n10

Bozzone, Matt, 93

Brennan, Timothy, 90

brinkmanship, 126n10

British empire, 31

Britton, Hannah, 103–4

Brown, Clifford, 17

bullying, 55, 94

Calvin, Fred, 37–38

Capital (Marx), 38

capitalism, 65

Capitalism and Modern Social Theory (Giddens), 26

Caporaso, James, 24, 25

Survey of Jazz course, 89
Sweet Honey in the Rock (activist musical group), 77
Switzerland, Geneva, 11–12
syllabi, 25
Syracuse, New York, 29
Syracuse University, 23, 30–31; Assistant Dean of, 37; department chair advice at, 32; mentoring program at, 40; team teaching at, 33–38; tenure process at, 39

"Taboos of the Teaching Vocation" (Adorno): debarbarization in, 107; taboo definition in, 104; on teachers, 104–7
Tamar (student): on *King Leopold's Ghost*, 110–11; writing of, 108, 109
Taylor, Catherine, 81
TB (friend and professor), 78
teachers, 6, 19, 78, 81; Adorno on, 104–7; corporeal punishment of, 106; criticism of, 14; desire of, 7, 14; as imperialists, 4–5; inquisitor for, 25; invisibility and visibility of, 35; love from, 100; from Somalia, 35; students dynamic with, 7, 32–33, 69n11, 89, 94, *94*, 95; theoretical application ratio of, 94, *94*, 95; unfairness ontology of, 105. *See also* academics; *specific teachers*
teaching assistants, pro bono, 89, 90–91, 92–93
"Teaching is Impossible" (Inayatullah, Naeem), 120
team teaching, 33–38
Ten Commandments, 20
tenure, 39, 42–43

Terence Fletcher (fictional character), 94, 95, 95n7
Theories of Exploitation course, 65–66
therapy, 103
Things Fall Apart (Achebe), 29
Thiong'o, Ngũgĩ wa, 29
Third World, 11; First World compared to, 73–74, 110; Inayatullah, Naeem, role as, 73, 95, 96
Thucydides, 6
Todorov, Tzvetan, 19, 75
To Know as We are Known (Palmer), 100–102, 103
Toktogulov, Kadyr, 62–63
Tom Crick (fictional character), 112–14
Tounkara, Djelimady, 54
tragic sensibility, 2
transference: Chamon on, 120, 120n3; Lacan on, 119–20; love as, 120, 120n2, 121
trust, 66
"Tuku," 83, 84
tuning, 87
Turner, Judith, 11–12

Understanding Capitalism course, 76, 81–82
United States (US), 5; Badaber Air Base use by, 10; economic probabilities in, 67; hatred toward, 65. *See also* imperialism, US
Universal Rules of conversation, 56
University of Colorado (CU), 24, 25, 27–28
University of Denver, 26, 73
US Embassy, 84
USSR, 62–63